BBC MUSIC GUIDES

BARTÓK CHAMBER MUSIC

BBC MUSIC GUIDES

Bartók Chamber Music

STEPHEN WALSH

BRITISH BROADCASTING CORPORATION

Contents

The music examples are reproduced by kind permission of the following:
Bagatelle, String Quartet No. 1 Editio Musica, Budapest; String Quartets
Nos. 2–5, Violin Sonata No. 2 Universal Edition (London) Ltd; String
Quartet No. 6 © copyright 1941 by Hawkes & Son (London) Ltd, reprinted
by permission of Boosey and Hawkes Music Publishers Ltd; Sonata for Two
Pianos and Percussion © copyright 1942 by Hawkes & Son (London) Ltd,
reprinted by permission of Boosey and Hawkes Music Publishers Ltd.

Published by the
British Broadcasting Corporation
35 Marylebone High Street
London W1M 4AA

ISBN 0 563 12465 2

First published 1982

© Stephen Walsh 1982

Filmset in Great Britain by
August Filmsetting, Warrington, Cheshire
Printed in England by
Hollen Street Press, Slough, Buckinghamshire

Introduction

Although Bartók's published chamber works are not particularly numerous, they loom so large in any consideration of his stature or development as a composer that one needs make no apology for treating them as a separate entity. The six quartets alone would furnish material for a far more extended study than the present one (and have in fact done so, in the shape of János Kárpáti's excellent if rather technical *Bartók's String Quartets*, published in an unfortunately poor English translation by the Budapest foreign language publishing house, Corvina Press). The quartets are not only a remarkable series of masterpieces in themselves, but since they cover almost every important stage of Bartók's mature working life they open a unique window on his artistic growth. On the whole he seems to have written quartets in a spirit of reflection and absorption, and away from the brutal practical necessity which compelled him to write piano music for his own concert repertoire (though he also used the piano, as Schumann did, for experimentation). This partly accounts for the greater range of the quartets: their intellectual daring, their great subtlety and variety of form, their consistent quality of finish and self-containedness. Perhaps it also explains why the most highly developed of them are also the hardest to appreciate on first acquaintance. Bartók was certainly not afraid of cerebration, and his quartets continue the late-Beethoven tradition of intellectual concentration and ruggedness: the refusal to compromise logic in the interests of beauty or emotional indulgence. Though Bartók's quartets often are beautiful, and (as I hope to show) certainly are emotional, one cannot hope to enjoy or understand them if one insists that music must before all else charm the ear.

The First Quartet was the earliest of Bartók's chamber works to be published during his lifetime. But it is not surprising to find that there were several previous chamber-music essays for a variety of instrumental combinations, two of which – a Violin Sonata in E minor (1903) and a Piano Quintet in C major (1903–4) – have been published and recorded since his death. Himself a pianist, a child prodigy (or nearly so) and the son of accomplished amateur pianists, he naturally composed exclusively for his own instrument in childhood. But after his widowed mother settled in 1894 in the Danubian city of Pozsony (at that time part of Hungary, but now Bratislava in Czechoslovakia), the 13-year-old Bartók found himself in demand as pianist in social music-making, and it is from this period that his earliest attempts at chamber music date. A sonata in C minor, for violin and piano, survives from 1895, and already shows unexpected freedom in the handling of conventional forms as well as a certain natural fluency in writing for the violin, though the piano part, oddly enough, is square and overwritten. The actual idiom is still, if anything, pre-Romantic. Bartók included this sonata in a list of his works which he drew up, probably in 1897 and 1898, a list which also mentions a pair of quartets written in 1896 (whether or not with piano we do not know as no music has survived), a piano quintet in C written the following year but also lost with the possible exception of a fragment of the slow movement, and two works which have come down to us practically complete, a violin sonata in A major (also 1897) and a piano quartet in C minor (1898).[1]

The advance shown by these two works in both style and technique is remarkable. By now Bartók is well into his Brahms phase under the influence of the over-riding Viennese taste of the day, which also ruled nearby Pozsony. The sweeping piano parts, succulent harmonies and rather heavy development sections proclaim the music's Germanic roots; and it is amusing that the composer, who had neither German nor aristocratic blood, signs himself 'Béla von Bartók' on both scores. (It would have been more than his life was worth to present himself in this form in anti-Austrian Budapest six years later, at the time of the 1903 sonata and quintet.) But in any case there is still no individual voice, whatever the assurance and technical maturity of the music. A string quartet in F major, completed in January 1899 and apparently shown to the Budapest piano professor, István Thomán, at the time of Bartók's acceptance for the Budapest Academy that year, likewise displays little individuality. A year later Bartók complained to his mother that Thomán regarded these instrumental works as too ambitious and advised him to 'attempt simpler things, songs for example'. Presumably because of Thomán's bad opinion, Bartók seems to have abandoned yet another piano quintet, though again there are fragments which almost certainly belong to the work.

Of course one is hardly astonished that a student of eighteen, however talented, has not yet found a creative voice of his own. But for Bartók the problem was to persist for a discouraging time.

[1] Full details of Bartók's juvenilia are given in Denis Dille: *Thematisches Verzeichnis der Jugendwerke Béla Bartóks 1890–1904* (Budapest, 1974).

During his student years in Budapest a succession of overpowering influences, mainly from the progressive German school, continually threatened his own nascent personality, and this at a time when student feeling in the Hungarian capital was increasingly xenophobic and nationalistic. Bartók was swamped by Wagner and Strauss at exactly the time when he would have liked to evolve a specifically Hungarian style. In the *Kossuth* Symphony, for instance, an essentially Straussian manner has to serve in celebration of the great nineteenth-century Hungarian patriot. And Brahms and Strauss are still the most obvious influences on the two large chamber works Bartók wrote at the time of *Kossuth*, the Violin Sonata of 1903 and the Piano Quintet of 1903–4. Both are superficially dominated by the rich Brahmsian textures for which Bartók had already shown a liking, though the harmonic language has a new flexibility derived from the young composer's intensive study of Strauss's recent symphonic poems.

But there is also in this music the glimmerings of something newer and more personal which, though it also owes something to the advanced harmonic practices of Strauss's *Zarathustra* and *Heldenleben*,[1] has a specific profile that is, in a sense, Hungarian. The three-movement Violin Sonata is conventional enough in outline: a sonata-form Allegro moderato followed by a set of variations on a simple diatonic minor theme (whose pedigree is decidedly Brahmsian), with a finale in the accepted manner of the rondo *all'ungherese*. But the Hungarianisms of the music go beyond the mere aping of a few linguistic courtesies. In the variation movement especially Bartók not only imitates the typical sound of the Hungarian gipsy band, with its rippling cimbalom arpeggios and cadenzas and its violinistic bravura, but he also actually uses certain oddities in the so-called 'gipsy scale', which to the nineteenth-century *pasticheur* were no more than exotic detail, to give a new dimension to the tonal harmony. Thus, at times, a wedge is inserted between the different lines of the music, forcing them into strange expressive contortions and unexpected clashes. The result is very different from anything in the Romantic repertory of Hungarian *pastiche*, even from that of Liszt, who made a study of the sources and, as a Hungarian by birth, had the best of reasons for wanting to

---

[1] Bartók's first movement contains a fugue based on a twelve-note theme evidently inspired by the *Wissenschaft* fugue in *Also sprach Zarathustra*, which Bartók heard for the first time in 1902.

absorb them into his own style. Bartók was later to make such absorption the very basis of his mature style, but with a fundamentally different raw material. The Hungarian elements in the Violin Sonata, like those of Bartók's other works up to about 1907, belong not to an authentic folk music or peasant tradition, but to a largely artificial and more or less recent urban tradition dating apparently from the middle or end of the eighteenth century and in large measure the creation of cultivated musicians. To this tradition belong the so-called *verbunkos* ('Werbungs') recruiting music of the Austrian army, the *csárdás* dance idiom, and the almost exclusively instrumental style of the gipsy bands who played (and still play) such music. After his discovery of Hungarian peasant music in 1904–5, Bartók concluded that the *verbunkos* style on which the Hungarian manner had up to that time been based had no validity as folk music, though he never rejected it as an authentically Hungarian phenomenon and, as we shall see, occasionally returned to it in his own music. His objection to it as the basis of a national style was that it was a composed, rather than evolved, music; and he seems to have mellowed in his attitude towards it after discovering that elements of it had penetrated, by a kind of osmosis, into the actual folksong of some Hungarian districts.

The Piano Quintet, though also flavoured with these romantic Hungarianisms (particularly in its last two movements, which have the character of the standard *lassú-friss*, slow-fast, sequence of the *verbunkos* and *csárdás*), uses them rather less boldly than the Violin Sonata. The composition of the work is masterly, and we can well understand that, having completed such a score, Bartók felt that his apprenticeship was over and that he could afford to start a 'definitive' numbering of his subsequent works (his next work, the *Rhapsody* for piano, was given the opus number 1, and the Scherzo for piano and orchestra was at once Op. 2, though not in fact published until 1961). But in tone of voice the Quintet is still heavily indebted to conventional models; the Scherzo, dazzling and vigorous as it is, is almost pure Brahms, while the harmonic treatment in the Adagio is Straussian to the point of anticipating Strauss's own use of chords in such passages as the 'Presentation of the Rose' music in *Der Rosenkavalier*. A more fruitful influence is that of Liszt, who seems to have inspired the cyclic technique of thematic transformation by which Bartók links the four movements of the Quintet. Since we find cyclic methods of one kind or another in all of Bartók's string quartets and in many other works as well, their appearance so early on may be regarded as prophetic. But such devices were the stock-in-trade of the late Romantic composer, who used them as much to lend variety to a limited supply of ideas as to give real coherence to his architecture. For Bartók, later on, it was the structural, or architectural, possibilities of the method which came to have particular appeal.

The Piano Quintet was completed in July 1904, and had its first performance in Vienna, with Bartók himself as pianist in November of that year. A Budapest performance, planned for the following month, had to be abandoned because of the work's technical difficulties (according to Bartók the Vienna performance itself had come close to breakdown on several occasions), and the Quintet was not heard in Hungary until March 1910, when it figured on the same programme as the First String Quartet (itself having its first performance) and the piano *Bagatelles*, Op. 6. Like Schoenberg at about this same time, Bartók found that his romantic younger self was a severe hindrance to the appreciation of his later and more experimental manner, and this probably accounts for his somewhat equivocal attitude towards the Quintet, which he withheld from publication while carefully preserving the manuscript and eventually taking a copy of it to America with him in 1940. His affection for the work is not hard to understand. If not the most personal of his youthful works, it is certainly one of the most accomplished and gives us a remarkable sight of a great composer on the brink of self-discovery.

String Quartet No.1

Between the Piano Quintet and the completion of the First String Quartet early in 1909, Bartók's music begins to assume a new and provocative individuality. For all its mastery and distinction of thought, the Quintet could never be recognised on its own as the work of a creative genius of the first order. On the other hand the Quartet, which is in some ways a less assured piece of work, definitely suggests a personal vision and at least the beginnings of a technical apparatus specially designed to express it. During these years Bartók emerged as a modernist in his own right. Much of his work in 1907 to 1909 is a reminder that this was the time of Schoenberg's and Webern's first atonal experiments as well as of the start of modernism, as a general concept, throughout the arts. But Bartók knew nothing of all that. Naturally his musical sources were (with one or two important exceptions) the same as Schoenberg's, since he was brought up in the same tradition. By 1904, as we have seen, he was already well acquainted with the music of Brahms and Liszt, had made a careful study of Wagner, and knew Strauss's symphonic poems. But these models for a time stifled him. Plainly he needed a shock from outside the central European academic musical tradition, to enable him to reappraise that tradition in a way that was useful to him creatively. In fact he experienced three shocks, two of them musical. In the years 1904 and 1905 he discovered and began to collect examples of authentic Magyar folk music; in 1907, apparently for the first time, he got to know the piano music of Debussy. That same year, during a summer holiday at Jászberény, he fell deeply in love with the young violinist Stefi Geyer.

The impact made by this attachment on the sensitive and introspective Bartók has perhaps been underrated. His love was almost certainly not returned, and the affair, such as it was, was definitely terminated by March 1908. But its density, so to speak, can be felt in the rather heavily sublimated letters Bartók wrote to Stefi during this time. And above all it can be heard in the small group of works associated with the affair: the First Violin Concerto, which Bartók began at Jászberény and later dedicated to Stefi Geyer, the *Deux Portraits*, the last two *Bagatelles* for piano of Op. 6, and the First String Quartet.

Of these works, the Concerto is pre-eminently Bartók's love-offering. He wrote it for Stefi and, when it was finished (in February 1908), he sent her the manuscript, which she subsequently withheld from performance with the result that the music only became known in its original form after her death in 1956. The two movements, as Bartók told Stefi by letter, were contrasted portraits of her: 'the idealised' and the 'lively, gay, witty, entertaining' Stefi respectively. But Bartók also intended a third portrait, significantly, of the 'cool, indifferent, silent Stefi Geyer' which would be, he said, 'hateful music' and which he finally decided to exclude at least from the Concerto. It seems probable, however, that he composed this 'hateful' movement soon afterwards as the acid waltz 'Ma mie qui danse' which forms the last of the fourteen *Bagatelles* for piano, Op. 6.

In the score of this sardonic piece the Hungarian words '*szeretöm táncol*' ('my love dances') are inscribed over the theme which Bartók had earlier assured Stefi was 'your *Leitmotiv*' and which figures prominently in the two movements of the Concerto. As if to confirm the link, the theme is also quoted near the end of the previous bagatelle, a funeral march subtitled 'Elle est morte', under the Hungarian label '*meghalt*' ('she is dead') – see Ex. 1 overleaf. In about 1911, at a safe distance from the Stefi Geyer affair, Bartók made an orchestral transcription of the fourteenth bagatelle and paired it with a slightly altered version of the Concerto's first movement to create a distinct work, the *Deux Portraits* ('Ideal' and 'Grotesque').

The First String Quartet is connected more obliquely with these passionate avowals. Bartók may have sketched out some of its themes during that same summer holiday at Jászberény, but otherwise it can only be related to the Geyer affair by internal evidence. The Quartet opens with a free canon between the first and second violins whose first four notes (taking the two parts as one) make up a pattern closely related to the second movement theme of the Violin Concerto. Bartók himself pointed out the connection to Stefi Geyer, calling the theme 'my funeral dirge', a description which calls to mind the lapidary thirteenth bagatelle. But Bartók did not explain that this four-note pattern, in its quartet form, is simply a dialogue version in the minor mode of the Stefi Geyer *Leitmotiv*, as can be seen in Ex. 1 overleaf.

Read as a melody, these notes crop up fairly often throughout the work, though more as a characteristic pattern than as a definitive motive. But János Kárpáti has observed that the chord formed by the four notes (a seventh chord in the minor, in third inversion) is fundamental to the opening movement, and is referred to several times through the independent motions of the four instruments. It is worth adding that seventh-chord patterns of this kind, made out of piled-up thirds, are a commonplace of Romantic music in its dying years (see, for example, the recurring fanfare figure in the first movement of Mahler's Third Symphony, which even uses the same 'snapped' triplet rhythms as Bartók's 'Ma mie qui danse'). The unresolved seventh in what is otherwise an ordinary common chord has an extraordinarily yearning effect; and this yearning romanticism is decidedly a feature Bartók's First Quartet shares with the other works of the Geyer epoch.

The influence of Wagner here is obvious, again particularly in the

Ex.1

(a) Bagatelle, Op. 6 no. 13
   (Lento funebre)
   (meghalt - - - - -)

(b) Bagatelle, Op. 6 no. 14
   (Presto)
   (Szeretöm táncol . . .)

(c) String Quartet No. 1 (opening)
   Lento
   Violin I

first movement (as in the slow first movement of the Violin
Concerto/*Deux Portraits*), and parts of the second. Bartók had been
familiar with Wagner's music since his student days, and since its
impact is nevertheless not strongly felt in his own music up to 1907
the sudden *Tristan*-esque flavour of the works conceived in that year
may reasonably be attributed to the emotional turmoil Bartók was in
at the time. But a qualification is needed. The melodic style of the
Quartet's opening may be close to *Tristan*, with the same reaching
chromaticism and the same tense preoccupation with auxiliary notes
at the expense of strong notes of resolution; but its contrapuntal
technique, in which the free-moving lines seldom pay rigorous
attention to any fixed harmonic framework, is rather closer to the
work of a later German composer not much admired in Britain but
whom Bartók certainly studied in 1907 and visited in Leipzig in the
early summer of that year: Max Reger. Whether or not it was Reger
who gave Bartók the idea of writing once again in the contrapuntal
medium of the string quartet we do not know. In any case, no one

could deny the powerful emotional significance of the First Quartet, and this can hardly have been suggested by Reger, or any other composer.

Bartók finished the Quartet on 27 January 1909. Apart from the sketches made in 1907, it had taken him almost a year to write, as we can deduce from a reference to the work in his last letter to Stefi Geyer (March 1908).[1] But it was a year much interrupted by trips abroad. During the summer he travelled in Germany, Switzerland and France, and later in the year he made a folksong-collecting excursion to Transylvania (still at that time part of Hungary). A note at the end of the score records the exact date of completion, and the following day Bartók wrote to his friend, the pianist Etelka Freund: 'I am happy to announce that the quartet got itself finished yesterday and would be pleased to visit you on Saturday evening (in my company). Would you be kind enough to receive it? If not, then perhaps on Sunday, after lunch . . .' Kárpáti conjectures that this led to a piano run-through whose success prompted the newly-formed Waldbauer-Kerpely String Quartet to take the work up. It may equally be, however, that Bartók showed the score to the violinist Imre Waldbauer at the Academy of Music in Budapest, where they both taught. According to Kodály's biographer, László Eösze, the Waldbauer Quartet was formed at the instigation of Kodály and Bartók expressly to perform the string quartets in a joint concert they planned for early 1910. Both composers were having trouble persuading established musicians to perform their chamber works, though in 1909 Bartók's earlier orchestral music (notably the two suites Opp. 3 and 4 and the 'concerto' version of the piano *Rhapsody*, Op. 1) was beginning to make slow progress against the tide of conservative opinion. Unfortunately these works were all in Bartók's pre-Jászberény Romantic style, whereas the Violin Concerto was, as we have seen, withheld and not a note of it performed until Waldbauer himself conducted the first *Portrait* in February 1911. Thus when the planned Kodály-Bartók concerts (two of them) took place in March 1910, few listeners were prepared for the greatly altered if still Romantic idiom of the First Quartet, and fewer still for the experimental and modernistic posture of the piano *Bagatelles* and first *Romanian Dance* (Op. 8a), which Bartók played in

[1] According to information furnished by her to Denis Dille, and quoted by János Kárpáti: *Bartók's String Quartets* (Budapest, 1975), p.173.

the same concert. On the whole the music was greeted with incomprehension and hostility. In revenge, later Hungarian critical opinion has unanimously dubbed this concert, and the Kodály concert two evenings before, 'the double birthday of modern Hungarian music'.[1]

At first sight the music itself hardly supports such a label. It is true that the *Bagatelles*, with their tentative essays in bitonality and dissonant chord-streaming (see, for instance, nos. 8 and 11) and their vigorous use of a keyboard style based exclusively on the melodic, decorative, and rhythmic mannerisms of folk-music (a style taken up more fully in the *Romanian Dances*), are the earliest examples of conscious modernism in Hungarian music. The neophiliac Busoni greeted them with rapture when they reached him in Berlin in 1908. But these pieces are still somewhat limited in range, and in technique frankly experimental. On the other hand, the more richly developed and personal First String Quartet retains strong links with German romanticism, whereas a divorce from Germanism in all its forms was, and still is, a prime condition of Magyar cultural autonomy.

Nevertheless Hungarians are right to attach such importance to this quartet, since it contains the seeds from which the great Bartók quartet oeuvre grew, and the quartets are, by common consent, the pillars of Bartók's creative work and the cornerstones of twentieth-century music in Hungary. This has nothing to do with nationalism as a phenomenon of style. Bartók's quartets continued to refer to German models long after they had shed the last vestiges of Wagnerian romanticism. At the same time the French influence, which anyone can hear in the First Quartet, may still be traced, in a much less easily recognisable form, in the Fifth and Sixth. As for folk music, the First Quartet plainly derives material from Bartók's collecting trips, in the form not of direct quotations (which he rarely used in his chamber or orchestral works) but of clear idiomatic references, often at critical moments in the scheme. Such references come and go, like characters in a play, and hardly yet form a constant factor in Bartók's style; in the later quartets, by contrast, the folk influence was absorbed in various ways, and direct allusions are comparatively rare. But precisely because the Hungarianisms in the First Quartet are pronounced and emerge from a context which is not in the least Magyar, it is possible to gauge here the relationship between the autochthonous and purely personal elements in Bartók's

[1] László Eösze, *Zoltán Kodály, his life and work* (London, 1962), p.19.

maturing style. From this it would seem that many of the chromatic oddities and acerbities of that style were Bartók's own interpretation of the Liszt – Wagner – Strauss tradition. Part of their individuality comes from the incisive rhythmic articulation. In nineteenth-century music, rhythm was typically subordinate to harmonic motion and tended to be governed by harmonic phrase-lengths and the position of the cadence, which is why the increasing vagueness of tonality in late Romantic music was often accompanied by a loss of rhythmic identity. Bartók, however, introduced rhythm as a factor independent of harmony, using it to articulate textures that were less and less controlled by harmonic logic and more and more by tonal centres whose sole logic was that of melody or which might even at times function quite arbitrarily, as they seem to do, for instance, at the start of the Finale of the First Quartet.

The ebullient, dance-like rhythms of this music may well have disturbed its early audiences, who were accustomed to think of the string quartet as a vehicle for the urbane discussion of lofty and subtle thoughts. To see just how false this hermetic view of the quartet is, one has only to examine the works of Beethoven, Schubert and Dvořák, whose quartets are full of vigorous dance rhythms. But Bartók's First Quartet already contains an important new ingredient: namely, the sheer aggressive brilliance, at times bordering on violence, of its rhythmic treatment. So far as I know, this feature is without precedent in the quartet literature, and was presumably suggested by the rhythmic exuberance of Hungarian folk-music. But, as with the influence of Reger, the mere suggestion cannot explain the astonishing expressive force with which Bartók invests this aspect of his music. There are even times (Second Quartet, second movement; Third Quartet, coda; Fifth Quartet, first movement) when rhythm seems to carry almost the entire idea-content of the music, with pitch and timbre changing largely to articulate the rhythms – a dramatic reversal of traditional roles. The character of such writing is not unlike Bartók's percussive approach to the keyboard which reaches its apogee in the Sonata and *Out of Doors* suite of 1926. Those who heard him play the piano tell us that when he sat down at the keyboard – a shy, reserved, introspective and slightly built man – he would seem suddenly galvanised into a ferocious activity. This account is also peculiarly apt to the contrast between slow and fast music in the quartets (the Third provides perhaps the best example). Nobody seems to have thought of treating the string quartet percussively before Bartók, and ever since the First Quartet was performed he has been accused of writing unidiomatically for the medium. What this criticism means is that Bartók expanded the quartet medium far beyond what had previously been regarded as its boundaries, and did so in a way which many listeners have found unsettling. As regards what cannot be played, or what is ineffective when played, by a string quartet, Bartók never wrote anything of the kind, at least if we may judge by the best modern performances.

By no means every aspect of the First Quartet, however, looks forward to later works. If the Finale, with its brilliant rhythms and graphic folksong allusions, contains at least the unblended ingredients for Bartók's most powerful and individual allegros (such as the first movements of the Fourth and Fifth Quartets), the slow first movement presents a type of music to which he never returned. The peculiar intensity of this movement, as we have already seen, derives from its association with the Geyer affair. In fact, it seems to have been written as the affair ended. Bartók called it 'my funeral dirge', while Kodály, perhaps thinking of the way in which the whole piece gradually wakes up from its leaden, nocturnal opening, used the suggestive phrase 'return to life'. Certainly the movement is heavy with emotional meaning. At times the straining chromatic lines and the sumptuous harmonies into which they settle (Ex. 2) come close to the Schoenberg of *Verklärte Nacht*, about which a contemporary remarked that it sounded 'as if someone had smeared the score of *Tristan* while it was still wet'.

Ex.2

The similarities with Schoenberg extend to the prevalence of large melodic leaps and to the curious liking for parallel thirds (major or minor) laid out against a chromatic or tonally indecisive melody. But most un-Schoenbergian is the occasional extension of this pattern into parallel triads (for instance, bar 44 etc.), a device which usually has a Debussian or Ravelian sound. On the whole this French influence is not yet fully absorbed, and its main significance here is that it shows that Bartók, unlike his Viennese contemporaries, was ready to use chords and scales for their colouristic or (in the Finale here) percussive value without regard to harmonic progression. The chordal 'pleasure principle', as he called it, was Debussy's earliest revolutionary concept. But in at least one respect Bartók's First Quartet applies it in a new and individual way. If we examine the two-part violin writing in the opening bars, we find that while the individual lines are fully chromatic (almost, indeed, twelve-note rows), the canon, or pseudo-canon, is organised in such a way that triads continuously result. Thus the first three notes briefly sound F minor, and in bar 3 the triads of B major, B minor and G major are clearly suggested.

This use of tonal vocabulary, so to speak, without tonal syntax is a French idea, but Bartók makes it middle-European by applying it in a context that is still German and expressionistic: close in fact to Reger. Throughout the First Quartet there is thus a curious but often beautiful equipoise between rich chromatic melody, occasionally harmonised in traditional fashion, and what amounts to a purely static type of harmony where the chords either run parallel to the melody or supply a fixed and motionless pedal beneath it. In the first movement the former type of writing predominates in the con-trapuntal first and last sections (bars 1 to 32 and 53 to 71), while the middle section, which is essentially non-chromatic, mainly displays the latter type. But in none of this music is there any question of key. Bartók uses tonal centres and references to suit the needs of the moment, usually allowing the melody (or one of the contrapuntal lines) to lead us from one to the next with only the most casual regard for tonal structure in the classical sense. In fact the First Quartet is often described as 'in A minor'. But there is hardly a sign of that key in the first movement; and although the Finale is rather more A-ish and ends firmly on A, the way Bartók reaches that chord, with a rushing whole-tone scale followed by an interlocking sequence of fourths (either of which could start or finish at any point), still leaves doubt as to whether A is the *necessary* tonal outcome of the work.

The truth is that such questions no longer have surpassing importance for Bartók. Not a single one of his string quartets is governed by key-structure, though they all use tonal centres to clarify their form, and indeed of all the quartets the First is the least explicit in that respect. This reflects its much greater fluidity of form and thematic treatment. The later quartets are all worked into tight formal symmetries, with the last degree of motivic economy and sophistication. But the First is neither symmetrical nor economical, and (like the Piano Quintet) uses motives less as all-purpose musical bricks-and-mortar than as referential themes in the Lisztian sense. Not that we have any idea what the themes actually mean. Perhaps there is a meaning when, at the height of the second movement's exposition (bar 94 etc.), the music inexplicably quotes the first movement theme (the one borrowed from the Stefi Geyer Violin Concerto) in a form it had assumed at the end of that movement; or when the Finale refers (also bar 94) to a seemingly irrelevant theme from the first movement. But what matters is that Bartók is still using a method of thematic cross-reference which is Romantic and programmatic in origin. In fact the First Quartet does have a kind of Berlioz *idée fixe* which pervades the second and third movements (Ex. 3). But it is only remotely connected with the Stefi *Leitmotiv*.

Ex.3 String Quartet No. 1
(a) 2nd movement, bars 18-19.

(b) 3rd movement, bars 5-6.

The First Quartet is not only asymmetrical as regards form, it actually undergoes a marked change of style and atmosphere from first movement to last. The opening, which is a free double canon (not a fugue, as is often said), has been compared with the slow fugal opening of Beethoven's C sharp minor Quartet, Op. 131, and certainly the contrapuntal writing has a skill and density which would have pleased the master. But emotionally we are worlds away here from the ethereal melancholy of the Beethoven Adagio (even though Joseph Kerman has described that movement, significantly in the present context, as 'Kareol-bleak').[1] On the other hand there *is* a Beethoven-like deftness about the transition from the first to the second movement, a passage which, according to Kárpáti, Bartók added after the Quartet was otherwise complete.[2]

Indeed as Bartók gradually quits the emotional darkness of the first movement he seems to enter more and more that luminous world where musical issues alone carry weight. The fugue which forms most of the development in the Finale is brilliantly energetic and self-assured, in the Beethoven manner, though its style is modern and probably shows the effects of the Reger study. It might appear that, in writing this work, Bartók literally composed himself into a new, personal and vigorous chamber-music manner, but for the fact that he is known to have sketched, if not written, the last two movements before he even thought of basing the first movement on the Stefi Geyer motive from the Violin Concerto. Already, in the abruptly curtailed reprises of the ternary first movement and sonata-form second, there are signs of that formal stringency which is the hallmark of at least the next four String Quartets and which, more than anything, supports the comparision with Beethoven. In the Second Quartet these qualities assume even greater importance.

String Quartet No. 2

The background to the Second Quartet is a good deal more obscure than that to the First. From Bartók himself we know only that he wrote it during the years 1915 to 1917, completing it in October 1917; there is no hint in his published correspondence or in the music itself of any emotional associations such as we found with the earlier Quartet. The war, of course, involved Hungary as one axis of the Austro–Hungarian Empire, and Bartók was affected both materially and spiritually like all his compatriots. But for his work the worst practical consequence of the fighting was that he was no longer able to make folksong collecting expeditions to more remote areas (for example, Romania was inaccessible as a neutral territory until 1916,

[1] Joseph Kerman, *The Beethoven Quartets* (London, 1967), p.330.
[2] But this passage, with its winding thirds, has also often been compared with the description of Kareol at the start of Wagner's *Tristan und Isolde*, Act 3.

and thereafter as an ally of the Western Powers). During the war he lived in Rákoskeresztúr, now an outer suburb of Budapest but at that time a village on the eastern fringes of the city, and from there he went collecting in the locality and even, in 1915, as far afield as Slovakia to the north. But for the most part he found himself at home, and with more leisure for composition than at any time in the previous ten years.

The effects of this enforced 'idleness' are plain to see in the list of his works. In the years 1915 to 1919 he wrote not only the Second Quartet but most of *The Wooden Prince*, the whole of *The Miraculous Mandarin*, the well-known orchestral *Romanian Folk Dances* (transcribed in 1917 from a piano suite composed in 1915), a large number of songs and part-songs, and a succession of piano works, including the *Sonatina*, the *Suite*, Op. 14, and the *Three Studies*, Op. 18. By comparison the years 1913 and 1914 are more or less blank. Many, even most, of these works are in one way or another based on folksong. The piano and vocal works include a large number of arrangements; and the bigger scores display for the first time a truly convincing fusion of folksong ingredients with personal expressive and technical mannerisms. The Second Quartet is the best integrated of all. Listening to this music, one feels at once that it must have been the product of a period of reflection and absorption. Unlike the First Quartet, it contains nothing half-digested and nothing incongruous. The earlier influences from other composers are now dissolved beyond recognition, and the folksong elements are so closely identified with the total expressive language that one is quite unconscious of any deliberate folksiness such as one finds in Stravinsky's *Les Noces* or Falla's *El amor brujo* – to name two of the finest twentieth-century folksong works, both of which happen to be exact contemporaries of Bartók's Second Quartet. This is emphatically the case with the first and last movements of the Quartet. Here the detachable folk ingredients add up to little more than one or two prevalent melodic intervals and certain ornamental devices. The folk *sound* of the music, so far as it exists, is just as much a general matter of timbre and harmonic procedure, both much cleaner and less luxuriant than in the First Quartet. The brilliant central Scherzo is admittedly more earthy, if only by virtue of its stamping drum-rhythms, the source of which is said to lie in an expedition Bartók made in 1913 to Biskra in North Africa to collect Arab folk-music. But even here, where the writing is predominantly of the melody-plus-rhythm type favoured by Bartók in his fast piano movements of this period, the peculiar richness and subtlety of his variation technique gives the music a complexity which the piano works mostly lack.

The fact is that, while the Second Quartet is an expressive – at times urgently expressive – piece of music, it has beyond that an intellectual rigour which is absent from the First Quartet and indeed from almost all Bartók's previous works. As a man he seems to have been a remarkable mixture of, on the one hand, deep sensitivity and powerful intuitive emotion; and on the other, social reticence and a liking for intellectual constructions and explanations. This comes out in his youthful letters (for instance, those to Stefi Geyer), in what we know of his life, and in his music up to about the time of *Duke Bluebeard's Castle* (1911). Indeed, his music continued to be fuelled by the conflict between passion and reason, and there is no doubt that the reconciliation of these potentially destructive opposites was, consciously or unconsciously, his most pressing creative need in the period 1910 to 1930. The Second Quartet is the earliest work to find the desired equipoise, and the fact that it should have been found in a string quartet naturally prompts comparisons with the great classical composers in the genre, in particular Mozart and Beethoven. The *moderato* first movement of the Second Quartet has indeed a Mozartian balance of grace and controlled eloquence. But more often in Bartók's quartets one thinks of Beethoven, especially the tempestuous Beethoven of the E minor and F minor Quartets, or, among the late works, the mercurial C sharp minor and B flat major. These quartets are the classic illustration of how the medium of four balanced strings lends itself to the working out of complex musical issues involving powerful expression held in check by contrapuntal and formal disciplines. With Bartók one is still more conscious of the stresses and strains. Often in his work, up to the late 1920s, the sheer violence and urgency of the expression threaten to tear apart the very fabric of the music, and most of his innovations in quartet sonority – the multiple-stoppings, special pizzicatos and so on – serve to release still more energy, still greater frenzy.[1] As these qualities intensify, so Bartók is compelled to balance them with increasingly strict organisation: tighter motivic and contrapuntal control, more elaborate formal symmetries. On the whole, the war of opposites

[1] Some of·these effects probably come from Berg, another composer in whom a passionate nature was offset by a love of intellectual constructions.

continues up to and including the final quartet, and the balance is always and essentially precarious; in which respect, of course, Bartók is very much a modern artist, and it would be a great mistake to press the classical comparison too far, however highly we may wish to praise his music.

In the case of the Second Quartet, the opposites are straight-forwardly represented by the first two movements, the one poised and lyrical, the other fiercely energetic. Thinking in classical terms, we might expect the Finale to restore the equilibrium of the first movement, perhaps with a rather freer motion. Instead the work ends with a rarefied and enigmatic slow movement, related themati-cally to the first movement, but seeming nevertheless to contradict all its expressive and formal characteristics. The thematic con-nections are by no means easy to detect, which naturally only helps deepen the enigma. Fragmentary reprises of this kind, suggestive of a man collecting up his broken belongings after being struck by a tornado, occur again in Bartók's chamber music – for example, in the 'Ricapitulazione della prima parte' in the Third Quartet. They have to be understood as an extreme instance of that love of varied reprise which invigorates Bartók's no less great love of formal symmetry and mirror repeats. The Second Quartet, indeed, is the first great implementation in his music of all these complementary techniques.

In outline, the first movement is a beautifully lucid example of that restless, continuously developing sonata-form which Bartók had already attempted, with fair success, in the First Quartet. The balance and function of the individual sections closely resemble those of the classical form. But there is little or no exact recapitulation, and no significant key-contrast. In their place, we find a tight fabric of motives, with everything evolving audibly from the first theme; and a carefully planned scheme of tonal centres, whose main role is to crystallise the argument at crucial points. These centres are quite unlike keys in conventional tonal music; they can submerge completely, and when they go they can be for all practical purposes completely absent, like submarines that have lost radio contact with land, whereas tonal music always maintains such contact, through its network of key-relations. In this first movement the most important centre is A (minor or major), with F sharp minor as an opposed centre: the built-in relationship between the two is shown in Ex. 4 – notice that the note A is the vital common denominator. But at the start of the movement neither centre is strongly present. If we took

Ex.4

the first violin melody on its own, we might feel that it at least starts
in A; but the accompanying chords contradict this so firmly that in
practice the centre is obliterated. Instead a series of other roots are
more or less vaguely implied. But the attentive listener will observe
how Bartók permits a peculiarity of the main theme – the falling
semitone between its third and fourth notes – persistently to displace
each would-be centre. For instance, at fig. 3 the falling motif
constantly translates C into B; at fig. 10 (the start of the development
section) E flat similarly slips to D:

Ex.5

Thus the tonal instability of these transitional or developmental
passages is closely bound up with their motivic content. Bartók is
then able to establish his more important centres by contrast at
moments where the motivic development has died down, or where
he wants to state comparatively new material. One such moment
comes at fig. 5, which most analysts call the second subject, though it
has in fact evolved without break from the first. Here a relatively
stable F sharp centre is helped by the absence at least of any overt
reference to the motive (though it is in fact present, as Ex. 6 shows,
and tries briefly to tug the music towards B flat).

Ex.6

At the end of this intensely lyrical passage, at fig. 9, the exposition closes in a mood of uneasy calm with a haunting codetta theme harmonised modally (*à la* Ravel) in F sharp strongly admixed with A. But later this same theme (somewhat modified) will clinch the whole movement (4 bars before fig. 21), firmly centred on A.

Thus the tonal centres and their conflicts frame the form and make it clear. But, unlike keys in tonal music, they do not in any sense control the argument. This is in the hands of the motivic texture. With Bartók, when we talk of motives, we usually mean melodic motives – short themes which contain the essence of the rest of the material. But the Second Quartet also shows Bartók infiltrating his motives, so to speak, into the harmony. We have seen how they can affect the tonal centres. Sometimes they actually supply the chords, as for instance at the very start of the work:

Ex.7

(a) First subject (transposed)   **(b) opening chord**
   (motive bracketed)

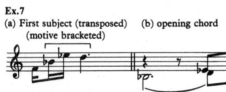

This is one of the not infrequent episodes where Bartók seems to hint at some kind of serial method, in which, as in Schoenberg, the chords and melodies are all derived from the same intervals. But they remain episodes. Much more of the time Bartók allows the four contrapuntal lines a certain independence of movement, governed mainly by motivic and textural considerations. In the Second Quartet there is not yet much sign of that ruthless linear freedom which makes the Third and Fourth Quartets such tough nuts for the new listener to crack. Here there is a good deal of traditional imitative writing, and parallel and contrary motion, often rather dissonant but always with a clear purpose and clear relationships.

Above all, Bartók's motivic work in the Second Quartet is marvellously plastic and in every way beautifully satisfying. A glance at the first few pages of the score will show how smoothly and economically he varies the opening idea so that it continually generates new but related ideas. The connecting link may be only one aspect of the original: its rhythm, or its melodic intervals, or even a general melodic contour derived from those intervals. Sometimes different ideas will fuse to form a new one. As a good illustration of these processes, it is worth comparing the main theme as re-capitulated (fig. 16 plus 7 bars) with its original form, and then following through the whole of this episode (up to fig. 19 plus 2 bars). It will be seen that this 'restatement' of the first subject is in reality quite new, and amounts to a clarification of the chief intervals in the theme, the perfect fourth and the semitone. The fact that these are also the predominant intervals in Hungarian folk-music may explain the slight ethnic flavour of parts of the movement, even though there is no specific ingredient of folksong. It undoubtedly explains the openness and sharpness of the texture compared with the First Quartet, where the more melting third still holds sway.

This openness of texture certainly does not arise from any thinness of scoring. Bartók has the four instruments in action almost the whole time, except where new sections are introduced by imitative writing. Yet despite the lack of rests there is skilful and pointed variation in the apparent density of the sound. Warm romantic doublings help confirm the more tonally stable episodes (figs. 5, 9, and 4 bars before 21). It remains a notable feature of all Bartók's later quartets that form is articulated by contrasts in texture and sonority.

This is no less true in the Finale of the present work. To isolate the various sections and identify their connections with the first movement presents no serious analytical problem. But what are we to make of the form as a whole? Writing to Endre Gertler about the Second Quartet in 1936, Bartók admitted that 'the last movement is the most difficult to define – in the last analysis it is some kind of augmented ABA form . . .' Mosco Carner, however, has suggested a comparison with 'the chain-like sequence of unrelated sections peculiar to a kind of Magyar music'. This hardly amounts to the specification of a form, but it does convincingly describe a type of assembly which we repeatedly find in Bartók's mature slow movements with their strongly marked formal divisions, cell-like themes, and elusive reprises. Nevertheless, it is not quite true to describe the sections as 'unrelated'. One can be deceived here by the extreme plasticity of Bartók's motivic developments which, in this very slow, fragmented music, have a certain quality of ellipsis. In fact, each link of the chain contributes to a process of growth towards a more sustained climax, which takes the place of a formal development section. After the climax the remaining links make up a definite, if inexact and compressed, recapitulation.

At the start the instruments (all with mutes) seem to be groping in the dark for some familiar thematic object. For instance, the three-note broken chord played by the violins in bar 2 is the same as the chord in bar 1 of the first movement, and the other broken chords are all variants of this shape. Quite soon (bars 3 and 5) the cello turns this chord into a melody, and at fig. 1 viola and cello begin to play around with the intervals in the first movement theme (Ex. 8), while the theme itself suddenly appears, distorted but perfectly recognisable, in the first violin two bars later.

Ex.8

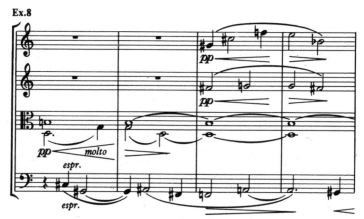

At the end of the section (4 bars before fig. 2) this same idea, again minutely altered, provides the bass to an important cadence-like motive in A minor, whose top line (viola) also recalls first movement material.

The next section (fig. 2 to fig. 4) starts by using this cadence-motive as a kind of ground bass, but then abandons it in favour of a purely melodic intensification based on the violin theme at fig. 2. The theme itself perfectly illustrates Bartók's motivic technique. It sounds quite new, and certainly strikes a new, plaintive tone. But in fact its elements are old. The rhythm and initial contour are those of the emerging cello theme in bar 5, while the notes include a substantial literal quotation from the first movement theme as reassembled by viola and cello at fig. 1 (Ex. 9). By gradually increasing the tempo, density and range of this melody, Bartók creates a climax which we can emphatically say has evolved from the opening bar of the movement.

Section 3 (fig. 4) now presents a fresh idea – apparently a second

Ex.9

(a) Cello, bar 6

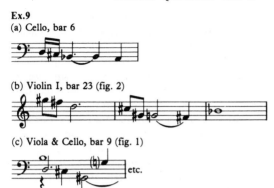

(b) Violin I, bar 23 (fig. 2)

(c) Viola & Cello, bar 9 (fig. 1)

etc.

subject. At first this is built on fourths (chords and melody), like the first movement theme, but it soon begins to prefer other intervals: a minor third in bar 2, major seventh in bar 4, and so on. Typically of Bartók, rhythm and contour provide the unity in what follows. Just after fig. 6 the smooth texture starts to break down into a dialogue between the first two notes of the fig. 4 theme in its minor-third version and the cadence-motive from earlier on. Something of a struggle develops, with the tempo again quickening and the texture filling out – the surging double-stop glissandi are a typical Bartókian way of raising the temperature at such a moment. Then a sudden hush brings us, paradoxically, to the real climax of the movement: in a passage of soft but tense polyphony (in two real parts) the four strings contemplate the new minor-third material, but in terms which also crystallise many earlier ideas: the wisp-like phrases which opened this movement, the minor thirds in the codetta theme of the first movement (fig. 9), and even the symmetrical up-and-down figuration of the first movement recapitulation (before fig. 17), with the fourths now compressed into thirds. After this the terse recapitulation (seven bars before fig. 9) has the feeling almost of a coda.

Whether or not one understands this broken and hesitant music as in some sense a reaction to the terrific thrust of the second movement is a matter of taste. Certainly the Allegro molto capriccioso is the most vigorous music Bartók had yet written for anything but solo piano (it compares with the Allegro barbaro and the second and third movements of the *Suite*, Op. 14, and anticipates the 'chase' music in *The Miraculous Mandarin*). But its vigour comes from high spirits as much as from any destructive impulse. The derivation from folk dance is obvious, in the stamping rhythms of the opening (drummed out pizzicato on the viola), the ornamental shakes and strange chromatics which colour the melody, and the prevailing simplicity of the texture – usually a melody with rhythmic accompaniment, which might, however, consist of dissonant chords (a pseudo-percussive device which Bartók had used as early as 1908, in the *Bagatelles*). In his letter to Gertler, Bartók called the movement a rondo. But it is hardly a rondo in the classical sense. The theme is constantly varied, in ways which might well suggest peasant performers getting more and more excited and daring.[1] And some of the episodes – if episodes they be – are hardly to be distinguished structurally from the onward rush of the theme itself, the main exception being the slightly whimsical slower episode starting at fig. 27, which forms a kind of brief trio section on its own.

Perhaps the greatest feature of this movement is the superb brilliance and resourcefulness of the string writing. Bartók derives unexpected resonance from the quartet by the free use of open strings (the D tonality/modality makes this convenient), and by fairly generous octave doublings. He also uses pizzicati and glissandi to sensational effect. Yet unexpectedly the most memorable touch is a delicate one: the needle-point *con sordino* writing in the *prestissimo* coda (after fig. 41), where the vision of peasant dancers momentarily blurs into a mere shimmer of light and sound. These innovations were to lead to still bolder experiments in later quartets.

The tonal language also repays study. Much of the music is devoid of chordal harmony. But the melodic figuring is enhanced by chromatics which are mainly decorative or colouristic – that is, they lend expression and piquancy to melodies which might otherwise not hold our attention for long. Bartók found that folk singers used chromatic inflections in very much this way, and his procedure here is basically an extension of their technique. Typically, however, he puts it to thematic use, as we can see in the equivocation between F natural and F sharp in the main theme,[2] which generates much of the motivic work later on.

[1] The energetic change from duple to triple time for the recapitulation (just before fig.34) is an early example of a device favoured by Bartók in his late works: see for instance the second movement of the *Music for Strings, percussion and celesta* and the outer movements of the Second Violin Concerto.

[2] An idea apparently derived from the equivocal nature of the third in peasant singing.

Music for Violin and Piano

The gap in time between the completion of the Second Quartet and the (apparently rapid) composition of the Third – almost ten years – is the longest between any pair of Bartók's quartets. Some writers have implied that this was because Bartók only wrote quartets when he wanted to sum up a period of stylistic change, and the change his style underwent in the early twenties was a particularly complex and radical one. The picture is irresistible of the great composer carefully mapping out his work schedule to ensure that his development is clear to university research fellows. But there were practical considerations too. The political atmosphere in Budapest was definitely unfavourable to creative work during the early and mid-twenties. Both Bartók and Kodály had been attacked for their 'incorrect' attitude to Hungarian nationhood, and in 1924 Bartók was quoted as saying: 'I have not been composing of late, I have neither the time nor the inclination.' Instead, he became increasingly involved in music-ethnology arising out of his collecting activities. In 1923 and 1924 he published no fewer than three folksong collections, complete with detailed critical apparatus and stylistic analyses. Moreover, his career as an international concert pianist and recitalist developed to the point where such composition as he was able to do was virtually confined to pieces for his own use and works written (like the *Dance Suite* of 1923) to special commission. Thus he wrote no string quartets because none were requested. Instead the period contains the last great burst of solo piano writing, the first of the three piano concertos, and the two important sonatas for violin and piano, written in 1921 and 1922 for concert tours in London, where Bartók played them with the Hungarian violinist Jelly d'Arányi in 1922 and 1923 respectively.

Taken as a group, these works constitute the most difficult and forbidding phase of Bartók's career. Not only is their music generally harsher and more dissonant than before, it also shows traces of formal disruption as compared with the beautifully clear and fluent structure of the Second Quartet. It seems that Bartók had once again fallen under a variety of external influences. We know that he heard and admired Stravinsky's early Diaghilev ballets, and their influence can be felt in the driving rhythms of *The Miraculous Mandarin* and the *Three Studies*. But it is likely that Bartók was also impressed by Stravinsky's novel cellular forms, and perhaps also by a comparable feature in certain late works of Debussy, particularly the sonatas for Violin and Cello with Piano. In addition the atonal (pre-serial) works of Schoenberg held a strong fascination for him at this period. The harsh, sometimes arbitrary-sounding, dissonances in which the First Violin Sonata abounds are peculiarly Viennese in their rather conscious avoidance of octave doublings and note-repetitions in consecutive chords. Bartók's melodic style, admittedly, remains quite un-Schoenbergian apart from a few passages of heavy octave displacement and a general atmosphere of expressionistic strain. But the frequent loss of tonal and harmonic focus undoubtedly contributes to the effect of formal disruption, as it tends to do in the early atonal works of Schoenberg and his colleagues.

The violin sonatas (the First especially) show the Schoenberg influence at its height. Even so, one could hardly call them derivative: their language and technique are Bartókian, and the flavour of both works still decidely Hungarian. Throughout this period Bartók was pursuing his interest in the chromatic oddities of Magyar folk-music, and there are examples in the sonatas of scales, arpeggios and melodic configurations which derive from them. The subject is rather technical. But it is worth noting that the absence of simple tonic-dominant relations is closely linked to the fact that most Magyar scales lack the perfect fifth in the tonic-dominant position. As in many types of folk music (Russian is another, hence certain features of Mussorgsky's harmony) the perfect fourth plays a much more important role, but with the augmented fourth (or tritone) also fairly prominent. A good illustration can be seen in the main violin melody of the Second Sonata. Bearing in mind that Bartók considered this melody (and the work) to be in C major, the lack of a G in the initial scale of the melody, and the prominent F sharp and F natural, are all significant.

An even more extreme case is at fig. 7 in the Finale, where the music dwells at some length on the same scale in reverse, transposed to G, with no sign of a D natural in the melody. Bartók developed a taste for the asperities of such scales; he made much use of the tritone (often treating it as an alternative or 'mistuned' dominant), and even extended the idea of semitonal shift from the fifth to the octave, and to the layout of chords (see, for instance, the Molto sostenuto just before fig. 3 in the Second Sonata's first movement, where the right hand of the chord seems simply to have been lifted by a semitone to add pungency and tension to the harmony). So a lot of the dissonance in these sonatas is Hungarianism as much as Schoenbergism.

Of the two sonatas, the first is generally considered the less satisfactory. Bartók himself is said to have taken against the opening Allegro appassionato, and would have liked to omit it when performing the work. If so, his reasons are not hard to guess. The movement is in sonata form. But unlike Bartók's best essays of the kind, it lacks true integration of material. From the start, the mood is rhapsodic and improvisatory (it even, oddly, suggests the rather overblown, theatrical style of the nineteenth-century gipsy fiddlers with cimbalom accompaniment), and not only are the ideas abruptly differentiated in character, but the two instruments have their own material to which they adhere strictly and without interchange. This gives the form a curious rigidity, very different from the highly mobile quality of Bartók's usual instrumental style, and not significantly offset by the rather feverish character of the ideas themselves.

With the second movement, an Adagio, we enter a completely different world as regards musical sound and texture, though still it seems that Bartók has not fully solved his problems of integration. Again the form is rigidly sectional, and again the two instruments are mainly preoccupied with their own material, delineated for the most part by actual or quasi solo writing. Thus, in the first part of the movement's ternary form, the rhapsodic violin solo is twice followed by a somewhat Debussian sequence of piano chords (to which, after a time, the violin adds a further rhapsodic descant). In the recapitulation (one bar before fig. 10) this same pattern is observed, with much modification in detail and rather less discontinuity of texture, but with its essential outlines unchanged. The middle section (from fig. 4) is identically constructed, but with more energetic material and a thicker fabric of sound (the violin 'solos' are now supported by the piano, but in the manner of a drum, with rhythmic ornaments but no deviation from the one basic pitch).

The movement in fact anticipates a type Bartók was to cultivate more and more in later works. Its obvious point (and this, of course, argues against his desired performing version of the sonata) is that it provides repose between the exertions of the first movement and the still greater exertions of the last. Form and content are therefore purposely somewhat static and contemplative, as in the similar Adagio of the Second Piano Concerto, the comparable slow movements of the Fifth Quartet (where, as in the Sonata, simple chordal harmonies lend an air of benediction), and above all in the great 'night-music' Adagios of the *Music for Strings, Percussion and Celesta*, the Sonata for two pianos and percussion, and the *Concerto for Orchestra*. Bartók seems, in all these movements, to be answering human activity with an objective calm imitated from nature; but in the First Violin Sonata the specific character of this contrast – so marvellously telling in the best of the later works – has not yet emerged, and it is the sheer contrast itself which is clearly meant to impress. Perhaps for that reason, the yearning violin solo and the serene piano chords have a slightly artificial, almost a disinfected, purity – the purity of tap water rather than spring water. And certainly the stylistic contrast with the first movement is disconcerting.

The rondo Finale presents a contrast no less abrupt. To some extent this hectic Allegro restores the strained atmosphere of the first movement, but in substance the music is more homogeneous and in form more coherent, despite the many showy and garrulous repetitions which fill out its considerable length. The piece is dominated by *ruvido* violin figuring and wild keyboard flourishes which again suggest a folk improvisation. Like the central 'rondo' of the Second Quartet (which it also resembles in idiom) it gets faster and faster, though with frequent pauses for breath. Yet this impetus is not matched, as it is in the Quartet movement, by great formal concision, so that in the end there is some feeling of excess, to which, as in the first movement, the sprawling harmonic idiom contributes.

It may be that the awkwardness of this First Sonata springs as much from difficulties with the medium as from a lack of stylistic integration. But if so, Bartók came to terms with them remarkably quickly. The Second Sonata already has a succinctness and balance that set it apart from its companion. There is still the same lack of explicit sharing of material between the instruments, and the texture is scarcely less dissonant. But the harmonies now resolve more consistently into patterns, emphasised by doubling between the pianist's hands or by textures uncluttered by seemingly arbitrary discords. Generally speaking, the sound is now harder, cleaner, and more precise. Its typical flavour derives from the tritone, and from semitone displacements of a directly bitonal (or bimodal major – minor) character, as for instance at figs. 4 and 7 in the piano part, or fig. 16 between violin and piano. But a crucial foil to these rather tense clashes is provided by the whole-tone scale, a scale which, because of its lack of semitones, gives the music an almost obsessively 'open' sound. Ex. 10 shows that most of one whole-tone scale is present in the opening theme.

Ex.10 Violin (piano omitted)

whole-tone scale

Since the theme dominates the sonata, the scale does so too; and Bartók uses this fact to obtain certain dramatic effects of colour based on whole tones. In the second movement, just after fig. 21, he writes a series of whole-tone clusters and scales in the piano; and at fig. 27 he introduces a fairly long section where the piano part is based entirely on whole-tone clusters, chords and scales played *leggiero* and producing a shimmer of sound behind the violin melody. This passage is laid out in such a way that the pianist's two hands play *different* whole-tone scales separated by a semitone – all at first within the same octave. In theory such a grouping is chromatic, since it gives every note between B natural (C flat) and the G sharp above; but because of the strict division into whole-tone groups it retains its open sound, quite unlike the 'saturation of musical space' which typifies the chromaticism in Schoenberg and Webern.

In such episodes, Bartók's eclecticism crystallises into individual shapes. Obviously Debussy lies behind this use of the whole-tone scale. But by giving the scale a chromatic context derived perhaps from the oddities of Magyar phraseology, Bartók distances himself once and for all from the placid and mysterious world of 'Voiles' or 'L'Ile joyeuse'. Something comparable may also be observed in his handling of the so-called 'barbaric' rhythms which occur fairly often in his earlier piano works but which seem to take on a new, menacing thrust in *The Miraculous Mandarin*, probably as a result of the influence of Stravinsky. In the Second Violin Sonata these rhythms revert somewhat to their original folk-dance character, while retaining much of the balletic subtlety and variety of the stage work. The ostinato keyboard rhythms are marked to be played softly and with a staccato or semi-staccato touch, so that the effect is light and mobile and the instrumental balance not strained.

Admittedly some of these tendencies can be found already (less well defined) in the First Sonata. But in one radical respect the Second Sonata differs from its companion: in the treatment of form. Perhaps already conscious of some dissatisfaction with the First Sonata, Bartók now takes the drastic step of doing without an opening Allegro altogether. Instead, he opens with a multi-sectional slow movement, much freer in form than the Adagio of the First Sonata, and runs this without a break into the dance Finale, a movement parallel in form and function to the Finale of the earlier work, but in effect both defter and more sparing. Moreover he links the movements thematically, in two main ways: first, by twice reiterating the first movement theme, as such, at salient points of the Finale (fig. 34, just before the recapitulation; and fig. 56, as a coda to the whole work); secondly, by deriving the main Finale theme from the first six notes of this theme, played backwards. Since both movements are rondos, and since – as we have seen – the themes also give rise to harmonies and textures, the result is in embryo a new kind of unity, a unity which has something in common with Schoenberg's attempts at this time to unify his music through the agency of a twelve-note row. But Bartók derived the idea not from Schoenberg, but from Debussy, whose work contains examples of similar procedures, without the actual note-ordering principle which was Schoenberg's crucial innovation. (Something more will be said about Bartók's use of this 'crude-serialism' in connection with the Fourth String Quartet.)

The form of the Second Violin Sonata suggests another and very different association. Its two-movement layout is exactly that of the standard *lassú-friss* ('slow-fast') sequence of the nineteenth-century *verbunkos* dance. That Bartók should now once more take an interest in this style is unexpected. (It reminds us perhaps of the 'gipsyisms' in the violin writing of the First Sonata.) He had apparently discovered elements of the *verbunkos* style absorbed into the instrumental folk-music of Transylvania, and this may have encouraged him to reintroduce some such elements into his own music. In any case the Second Sonata was to be the first of several works in *lassú-friss* form. Of these, by far the most important is the Third Quartet, which has a double *lassú-friss* plan. It also has other resemblances to the Second Violin Sonata: compare, for example, the violin theme in the Finale of the Sonata with the pizzicato cello theme which opens the second part of the Quartet. But also worth brief consideration here are the two Rhapsodies for violin and piano which Bartók wrote soon after the Third Quartet, in the summer of 1928.

The Violin Sonatas are a serious, if not wholly successful, attempt at a modern equivalent of the classical duo. That is, the instruments are opposed but equal. In the Rhapsodies, however, the violin takes the stage as a soloist, with piano accompaniment, for which reason both works have had success in orchestral transcriptions which Bartók himself made in 1929 – something which would be inconceivable with the Sonatas, despite the piano's occasional mimicry of other instruments.[1] The violin writing is not difficult in the 'strained' sense of the sonatas; but it is technically demanding and full of bravura. Since the pieces are entirely based on genuine folk tunes, it seems reasonable to suppose that Bartók intended a kind of stylised concert portrait of folk-music-making in the areas from which he derived the tunes (Transylvania, Romania, Hungary). In this he harks back in some sense to the nineteenth-century pasticheurs. But of course his own work is far more literate, far more sensitive and far less condescending. It may be noted how careful Bartók is to harmonise the melodies in a way that agrees with their own chromatic peculiarities, which incidentally plainly show the source of the more piquant oddities in the violin sonatas and other works. In the first theme of the First Rhapsody, it is pleasing to note the presence of both B natural and B flat in the melody on keynote G, in view of Bartók's own enthusiasm for this type of false relation (see, for example, the Second Sonata, first movement, fig. 7). As for the violin's ornamentation of the melodies, this may well have been suggested by peasant fiddling but undoubtedly also reveals some-thing of Bartók's exquisite sensibility. Even in the Second Violin Concerto there is little to compare with the decorative refinement of the second theme in each of the two rhapsodies.

Bartók's Rhapsodies have no pretension to subtlety of form. At bottom they are medleys of good tunes attractively presented, but with occasional references to more elaborate forms in the develop-mental treatment of a theme, or in an unexpected recurrence. The *friss* section of the First Rhapsody, for instance, concludes with a brief restatement of the main melody of the *lassú* – a curious recollection, in this very much simplified context, of the slow reprise which ends the Second Sonata. However, Bartók later made a version of this

[1] The cimbalom-like opening of the First Sonata is echoed by Bartók's actual use of that instrument in his orchestration of the First Rhapsody.

ending, to be used when the *friss* was performed alone – as he allowed that it might be.[1] Here a restatement of the first theme of the *friss* itself is substituted. There is in this an odd reminder of the Third Quartet, composed immediately before, in which both reprises occur, admittedly in a stylised form. Perhaps Bartók did not intend any such parallel in the Quartet. But we can certainly observe in this series of works – Second Sonata, Third Quartet, Rhapsodies – the development and refinement of one kind of formal preoccupation, before its rejection, in the Fourth Quartet, in favour of a richer and more elaborate pattern of symmetries.

String Quartet No. 3

In July 1927 Bartók, who was spending the summer at Davos with his wife, went to Germany to give performances of two of his piano works. He played the Piano Concerto at an ISCM concert in Frankfurt on the first of that month (this was the Concerto's première); then on 16 July he was in Baden-Baden playing the Sonata. The Baden-Baden concert was to provide music history with one of its more fruitful chance encounters, for it also included a performance of Berg's *Lyric Suite* for string quartet (not, however, its first performance, as Ujfalussy wrongly states; that was in Vienna the previous January). Although Bartók's correspondence, which refers to other music he heard in Frankfurt and Baden-Baden, makes no mention of the Berg work, it seems likely that he heard and was impressed by it. He had written nothing for string quartet for ten years. But within less than three months of this performance of Berg's masterpiece he had fully composed his own Third Quartet, a work which plainly shows the influence both of Berg's methods and of his expressive sonorities. The Quartet is dated September 1927. Its further history has a certain bizarre interest. Bartók submitted it (possibly in person, as he was touring in the USA from December 1927) for a competition sponsored by the Philadelphia Music Fund Society, and almost a year later, in October 1928 (after the completion of the Fourth Quartet), he heard that he had shared the first prize of $6000 with the Italian composer Alfredo Casella.

[1] Bartók's own recorded complete performances also use this revised ending, and that has become normal practice.

It would be hard to exaggerate the perspicacity of this award. The Third Quartet not only makes extremely novel use of the quartet medium, it is highly unconventional in design, elliptical in formal method, and sometimes brutally harsh in sonority. It is worth comparing it in these respects with Berg's *Lyric Suite* (composed the previous year), and also with another important string quartet of the same period, the Third Quartet of Schoenberg, composed in 1927. Both these quartets use the serial method, though the *Lyric Suite* for only some of the time. At the time it was widely assumed that serial/atonal music was more radical aesthetically than music such as Bartók's which, even at its most discordant, still referred obliquely to tonal centres. But this is not necessarily the case.

Schoenberg's Quartet is in fact a rather traditional-minded work, apart from its avoidance of tonality. Its four movements are broadly the conventional ones of nineteenth-century sonata-symphony usage, these forms are articulated in ways which are at least analogous to traditional procedures, and the writing for quartet, while masterly, is not markedly adventurous. I do not undervalue Schoenberg's brilliance in manipulating his series to produce a complete range of related motives and themes plus a coherent texture independent of key. But in all this he seems to be merely answering well-established needs, by overcoming the revolutionary elements in his language as if they were an unavoidable obstacle rather than the medium of a new way of thought.

With Berg this compensating mechanism is less noticeable. As always in his music, the expressive surface distracts attention from the radical procedures underneath. In the *Lyric Suite* both the number (six) and form of the movements is in varying degree unconventional. Moreover, their extreme contrasts of mood, texture and tempo, together with the mysterious quotations from other works and other movements, suggest that the underlying impulse is dramatic, or narrative, rather than symphonic. In fact, as George Perle and others have shown, Berg's compositional method is surprisingly self-conscious, with its use of palindromes, number symbolism, row-rotations and harmonic fields. But what mainly concerns us here is that Berg, unlike Schoenberg, acknowledges the new conditions imposed by the rejection of tonality in its traditional form; far from allowing his material to be limited by these conditions, he diversifies freely, mixing tonal with atonal, new with second-hand, free polyphony with counterpoint that is strict to the point of contrivance, development-type textures (in the Schoenberg manner) with static or revolving textures, lyric melody with passages based exclusively on contrasts of chord and tone-colour. Yet with all this radical mixture of elements, Berg is still consistently preoccupied with one great traditional virtue: beauty of sound. In the *Lyric Suite* there is much that is beguiling, much that fascinates the ear, and a few passages which seem, through excess of emotion, to risk ugliness. But there is never anything deliberately harsh or repellent. Indeed, it can fairly be said of all the three great Viennese serialists that beauty of sound remained for them an ideal, in no way dethroned by the rejection of tonality or the emancipation of the dissonance.

For Bartók, in his Third Quartet, this is no longer so. Here sounds that are coarse and grating are an integral part of the material. The work opens with a soft but penetrating dissonance which (like the chord at the start of the Second Quartet) outlines an important motive; and it closes with a violent series of discords whose role is apparently to end the work with a conventional gesture that is nevertheless apt to the stylistic context. (Significantly, Webern is reported to have said of Bartók's in some ways less strenuous Fourth Quartet, 'It is too cacophonous for me.') Of course Bartók was not the first to admit harsh sounds to his expressive language. In Paris such things had been commonplace since Stravinsky's Russian-period ballets, and by the early 1920s were almost regarded as a necessary proof of modernity, just as in America at the same time Varèse was evolving discordant sounds into a kind of neo-Impressionism for the mechanised society. But such aesthetic postures, whatever their value, had no interest for Bartók. As before, he was pre-eminently concerned with perfecting a coherent but energetic language and unified structures to contain the urgent expressive force of his ideas. If this involved an element of harshness, so be it; he had no special affection for academic good behaviour or traditional musical manners. Had he not found, among the peasants of rural Hungary and Transylvania, a warmth of friendship combined with an ebullient energy of musical culture? But in Budapest he had met with little but political manoeuvring and interference combined with entrenched views about music and a ludicrously abstract and doctrinaire nationalism.

Thus Bartók's Third and Fourth Quartets perhaps embody a protest, but it is a fundamentally private and almost involuntary one. On the musical side they certainly show the consequences of importing non-Western rustic mannerisms into the very Western and non-rustic medium of the string quartet. The harshness, in other words, is partly the result of translating rough, percussive, and perhaps mistuned sounds into a medium whose nature it is to be refined. But partly, too, it is the result of the intellectual and emotional complication of a melodic idiom designed to be elaborated mainly by ornament and varied repeat. Here Bartók is at his farthest from his Viennese contemporaries, technically as well as aesthetically. Where their material is all-embracing, fully chromatic as well as, in Berg's case, allusive, Bartók's is initially narrow, expanding only with effort. But the melodies are not only cramped, they are also brief. Bartók is able to extend them by such devices as repetition, sequence, or imitation between several instruments. But this remains the extension of something essentially small (Kárpáti uses the term 'micro-melody', which may suggest the phrase 'micro-polyphony' coined by a later Hungarian composer, Ligeti, to describe one of the procedures in his music). In the Third Quartet micro-melody leads, inevitably one may feel, to micro-phrases and micro-sections – but only in the slow movements. In the quicker parts Bartók's wonderful rhythmic sense ensures a more emphatic continuity.

A brief account of the form may help to show this difference. Bartók divides the Quartet into four parts, in the sequence slow-fast-slow-fast, with the third part labelled by the composer, in Italian, 'Recapitulation of the first part', and the fourth part labelled 'Coda'. In fact one quickly perceives that this coda is, to the same extent, a 'Recapitulation of the Second Part', though in both cases the term 'recapitulation' is misleading since the resemblances, such as they are, are resemblances of theme rather than structure. 'Continuation' would perhaps be a more accurate description. Bartók's terminology nevertheless indicates clearly enough that he felt the work to be in two movements whose final sections had become detached from the main body in each case. Why this should have happened is naturally an open question. In a romantic work one might interpret the *Ricapitulazione della prima parte* as a sentimental reminiscence in the manner of Liszt. But here the reference is at once too oblique and too factual to have any such significance. In purely formal terms, it seems that the first part arrives after some conflict at a point of temporary stability, from which the more vigorous and explicit second part can suitably launch itself, but that something remains unresolved in connection with the material in the first part. Later, when the energy of the second part is momentarily subdued by the disintegration of its themes, the original argument is resumed, in terms somewhat moderated but recognisably similar to those of the first part. This is followed in turn by a culminating resumption of the second part, with its themes triumphantly and conclusively reassembled. At each change our attention is drawn to the drastic contrast between two autonomous kinds of music: the one static and introverted, the other highly mobile and demonstrative.

These, as we have already noted, are a recognisable if stylised version of the *lassú-friss* sequence in nineteenth-century Hungarian music. But they also suggest a more serious duality, of the kind associated previously above all with late Beethoven. For instance, the fierce oppositions which open the string quartets Op. 130 and Op. 132 have something of the same quality, and there are more formal polarities which come closer to Bartók's arrangement in the double-variation slow movement of Op. 132 and the fugal Finale of the Á flat Sonata, Op. 110, where Beethoven's rather ceremonious Italian markings also curiously anticipate Bartók's. Joseph Kerman wrote of the contrasting sections of the 'Heiliger Dankgesang' in Op. 132: 'The two do not mix, they do not understand one another, and it is only by a sort of miracle that they do not wipe each other out or simply collapse. This is one measure of the seriousness of the musical contrast.' In Bartók's Third Quartet this threat of mutual destruction is almost tangible in the closing stages of the *seconda parte* (from fig. 41), where the texture starts to break down but steadies itself temporarily by clutching at a subsidiary thematic fragment from the *prima parte* (fig. 46, cf. *prima parte* three bars before fig. 11). The contrast is hardly at all diminished by certain more fundamental motivic links between the two parts; but these are presumably a crucial factor (Kerman's 'sort of miracle') in integrating the whole work at the unconscious level, so that when this fifteen-minute piece reaches its violent and abrasive conclusion we actually feel that the argument has been properly tied up, rather than merely conveniently terminated.

In fact the Third Quartet provides abundant evidence of Bartók's concern that the extremes of his personal expression should not jeopardise the unity and coherence of his work. The motivic organisation is more complete even than in the first movement of the Second Quartet, and there is now also extensive use of classical contrapuntal techniques such as canon and fugue with associated procedures (inversion, retrogression and so on). Possibly Bartók was influenced in this respect by Berg. The rigorous pattern of derivations in the *prima parte* certainly has a Schoenbergian feel. Yet the actual themes bear a surprising resemblance to those of the first movement in the Second Quartet, and are quite unlike anything in the music of the Second Viennese School. The main rhythmic nuclei of the two movements are almost identical, and there are distinct melodic similarities: for instance, the fourth is the most important interval in each, while chains of fourths – either pure or with a semitone gap – are prominent in both movements. The two most obvious differences (apart from questions of form) are that the expansive lyricism of the Second Quartet is absent from the Third; and that the harmonic images which occasionally emerged from the contrapuntal fray in the Second Quartet are now suppressed in favour of a free interplay of lines and a chord structure governed almost exclusively by motivic considerations.

Both these differences are the result of Bartók's insistence on unity; and there is a further consequence. Particularly in the slow music, the tight, self-referential character of the writing has the effect of turning the music so much in on itself that it loses onward motion. As a matter of fact the fast parts are essentially like this too, but are able to achieve motion through rhythm. In the slow parts, however, the tendency for the music to break off after each few bars is extraordinarily marked. Notice, for instance, how self-contained the first paragraph in the *prima parte* sounds (bars 1 to 6). The fact that there are motivic links between paragraphs does not of course in itself ensure continuity. What it means in this case is that the listener has the sensation of continually shifting position in order to view the *same* material from a new angle. In the process the material is apt to change its shape, to become more or less distorted, elongated or compressed, fragmented, reassembled, until the focus suddenly comes right and we hear the full theme in its most open and candid form (4 bars after fig. 11, Ex. 11 overleaf).

To achieve this, as one might call it, sculptural effect, Bartók brings to bear astonishing ingenuity in the handling of motives. As in the Second Quartet the materials are highly plastic. The first four notes in the first violin contain a rhythm and a melodic figure, while the next four repeat the rhythm and also repeat the melodic figure in inversion. If we take this melodic outline as a flexible unit, we can easily see how it gives rise to the more open figure (same rhythm) in

Ex.11 accel. al Tempo I ♩ = 88-84

bars 7 and 8, which later also forms the characteristic cell of the full theme at the end of the *prima parte*. Then at fig. 4 this same motive, played in canon by the viola and cello, supplies an ostinato accompaniment to what looks like a new theme but is in fact a compressed version of the original first violin melody, to a new snapped rhythm. We may also note that the four notes of the snapped-rhythm phrase (in the third bar after fig. 4) are simply the four notes of the very first chord in reverse. The connections are shown in Ex. 12.

Ex.12

(a) Violin I (bars 2–3)

(b) Violin I (bar 7)

(c) fig. 4 + 1 bar

(build-up of opening chord)

Within each short section Bartók treats these ideas with the same controlled freedom we remember from the Second Quartet. In the pseudo-canon starting at bar 6 he allows the imitations to expand and contract within quite wide limits: compare the viola entry at fig. 1 with the cello part which supposedly follows it a bar later, and then also compare this cello line with the original violin melody at bar 6. This apparent laxity not only gives shape to the individual sections, it also continually generates new ideas. For instance the tiny, self-contained section at *Tempo I* (after fig. 5) may not at once proclaim its kinship with the main theme, but we can trace that kinship back through the snapped-rhythm variant. In the new section the instruments play in pairs so arranged that the violins share the four notes of the original snapped figure in the first violin and the viola and cello share the four notes of the counter-motive originally played by the second violin. But the rhythm itself is quickly smoothed out into a quaver-crotchet syncopation, which then proceeds to supply the main rhythmic force behind the climax after fig. 7.

These procedures are traditional enough in themselves, and what gives the Third Quartet its special character is the rate at which Bartók varies his ideas. Everything it seems is stated in concentrated form, and so tension accumulates and within only two or three minutes of the start we are assailed by a climax of quite exceptional ferocity. Indeed the whole tendency of this *prima parte* is up-thrusting; notice the upward push of the melodies after fig. 1, after fig. 3, before fig. 6, and between figs. 7 and 9. Turning to the so-called 'ricapitulazione' we find a contrasting downward tendency, even though the material is still derived from the *prima parte*. Ideas which there reared menacingly, here droop submissively; even the fierce closing motives (after fig. 5), which all refer more or less directly to the *prima parte*, lack the assertiveness they had before. This is presumably because the *seconda parte*, with its explosive ending, has released the accumulated energy, leaving the 'ricapitulazione' to fill the largely formal role of stabilising the quartet's conclusion, so that it does not collapse under its own impetus.

I have already referred to the 'drastic contrast' between this slow music and the *allegro* music of the *seconda parte*. The change is marked by a rhetorical introduction with an expectant trill on the second violin and crisp folk-dance phrases on the cello, pizzicato and triple-stopped. The rise and fall of these phrases is further enlivened by more rapid semiquaver and demisemiquaver figures on the other strings, and from these the main dance theme of the movement soon emerges (fig. 3), still accompanied by the pizzicato cello and the violin trill. All these motives have their origins in the *prima parte* (especially in the passage after fig. 10). But their character is altered beyond recognition. The dance tune swings along effortlessly, with subtle cross-rhythms, many repeated notes, improvisatory extensions and expansions, as if we were really listening to a complex peasant performance in which the players were free to vary the tune according to certain set patterns, and in which the tempo gradually increased and the rhythm intensified as the excitement mounted. As in the *prima parte* Bartók achieves his effect with amazingly little material. Everything that happens is more or less directly a variation of the dance tune or its accompaniment. But Bartók tightens the screw by two means: first, by the introduction of contrapuntal subtleties, which disturb the natural gait of the dance-tune; secondly

by a simplification of the rhythm. Thus, for instance, at fig. 7 plus 2
bars the varied tune is accompanied by an inverted variant of itself
with the rhythms displaced by what is known as a rotation (in this
case taking the two semiquavers from the end of the first violin
phrase and placing them at the start of the second violin). The
unsettling effect seems to lead directly to the vital rhythmic
simplification, embodied in an important motivic variant at fig. 10
(viola and cello), which now drives forward in three-eight time with
a powerful syncopation but few irregularieties of barring until just
before the fugue at fig. 31. This variant is also treated canonically,
and it is about here that the music begins to lose its simple dance
character and to take on a more demonic urgency redolent of certain
passages in *The Miraculous Mandarin* or the Diaghilev ballets of
Stravinsky and Prokofiev. There are clear signs of disruption already
in the flailing semiquaver ostinatos after fig. 19. The process is
temporarily halted in the sparkling fugue on another variant of the
dance-tune, surely the best piece of fugal writing for string quartet
since Beethoven's Op. 131. But in the recapitulation to which this
leads (fig. 36) the movement never recaptures its dance flavour and
soon begins to fragment as Bartók typically compresses his material
into many fewer bars than it previously occupied. The extraordinary
glissandi at fig. 44 are a grapnic symbol of this disintegration. Such
fragments of material as survive (including the quotation from the
prima parte) are soon wafted away by a massive four-part trilled
chord, triple *forte* and *molto vibrato*.

Logically the coda might have followed at once. But, as already
suggested, Bartók must have felt that in the interests of stability and
correct proportion something else was needed, if nothing new or
substantial. When it does shortly materialise, the coda resumes the
dance rhythms of the *seconda parte*. But the pace is even faster than
before (one thinks of the *prestissimo* coda in the middle movement of
the Second Quartet), and there is soon once more a threat of collapse.
This time, however, there is no disintegration, and instead the
music's centrifugal energy is somehow turned round and, in the final
pages, binds the music into a ferocious unity.

Opinions have always differed as to the stature of this extraordinary work. Some critics feel that Bartók's abandonment of lyricism
was a self-conscious denial of his expressive needs, and that the
harshness and compression of the writing serve no end beyond that.
Others consider that the work, however forbidding, is a masterpiece

sui generis, a brilliant balance of animal vitality and intellectual reflection. It certainly appears that the Third Quartet was a successful and conclusive reconciliation of the various forces at work on Bartók's music in the 1920s, but while this is impressive in itself, and while it is hard to deny the music's vigour, cohesion and individuality, its emotional range is undoubtedly narrow compared with that of its two predecessors, as well as – more significantly – with that of its successors, to which we now turn.

String Quartet No. 4

By the time Bartók heard about the success of his Third Quartet in the Philadelphia competition he had, as we have seen, already completed the Fourth. According to the score, it was written between July and September 1928, while the result of the competition was published only in October. This means that for once Bartók proceeded to the next in his cycle of quartets without having the opportunity to check the previous quartet in performance – a process which we know from his correspondence with his publishers, Universal Edition, he regarded as an essential part of the act of composition.[1] While the prize was being judged the Third Quartet was effectively lost to view. But Bartók must have felt an urgent need to pursue the creative issues raised by that work. This is suggested not so much by the obvious and natural similarities between the two works as by their differences, many of which are in the area of formal pre-planning and so indicate a conscious search for suitable ways of framing smaller structural processes which themselves do not so markedly differ. The five-movement plan of the Fourth Quartet is so strikingly unlike the rather constricted binary scheme of the Third that it is tempting to exaggerate the purely stylistic change it embodies. But the more one studies the Fourth the more one feels its kinship with the Third, even though the new ground-plan allowed Bartók so much more elbow-room that, in the end, the Fourth inhabits a much richer and more diverse emotional world.

Bartók was far from being a conscious innovator where musical form was concerned. Throughout his life he was devoted to cyclic procedures not essentially different from those of nineteenth-century

[1] See Kárpáti, p.198 and footnote 145, p.279.

composers such as Liszt and Franck, while the forms into which individual movements fell were to be regarded, in his own view, in quite traditional terms. There is evidence of this in the formal analysis printed at the head of the Philharmonia miniature score which, according to Kárpáti, was written by the composer. The analysis is conventional to the point of obscuring certain basic facts about the music itself. But this is not to say that Bartók, as a composer, was uninterested in formal questions. From the start he tried to formulate his works so as to resolve their inner stresses and strains; and this led to some surprising results, such as the enigmatic finale of the Second Quartet and the interleaving of movements in the Third. In the Fourth Quartet he for the first time adopted a purely symmetrical arch structure of five movements, with the movements paired so that the finale 'echoed' the first movement, the fourth movement echoed the second, and the third movement formed an independent keystone to the arch. We find the same arrangement, somewhat intensified, in the Fifth Quartet.

Given the rather violent and 'expressive' character of much of the Fourth and Fifth Quartets, it seems reasonable to interpret the formal symmetries as a kind of counterbalance. This is certainly the effect of such procedures in Berg, where the relation is often a dramatic one expressing, as it were, the impotence and futility of passion. It would be going too far to try and explain Bartók's chamber music in such terms, despite the hint of fatalism in the late recurrence of the mournful first movement theme at the end of the Fourth Quartet, not to mention the famous 'con indifferenza' passage near the end of the Fifth, where the fierce main theme appears in the guise of an empty hurdy-gurdy tune. But Bartók was certainly looking for ways of containing the destructive element of expression in these middle-period works. The almost ruthless logic in the handling of small motives was probably an instinctive channelling of aggressive energy. But the formal logic smacks much more of conscious control. In the Fourth Quartet the parallel between the second movement scherzo (*con sordino*, chromatic, ABA) and the fourth movement scherzo (pizzicato, diatonic, ABA) is obviously contrived. And, turning to the form within single movements, the device of recapitulation – which is often what first makes the analyst think in terms of sonata form – is typically Bartók's way of reasserting command over music that has begun to dis-integrate from sheer centrifugal energy. We have already observed this in the Third Quartet (end of the *seconda parte*), and we can see it again in the first movement of the Fourth. As in the earlier work the form is quite clearly built up from tiny self-contained units, about two bars long at first though later their size varies more. And again these cells, while sharply differentiated in texture, are based on variants of the same motives, so that the music presents the appearance of a highly compact set of developing variations, across which certain broader lines can be drawn (for instance Kárpáti sees bar 14 and those following as the second theme, while Bartók's own analysis calls this 'transition'; in any case it is the sixth distinct section). The pattern continues, with varying density, until bar 60, where a reprise of Kárpáti's 'second theme' leads unexpectedly to a much broader composite melody which, for the time being, assumes the character of a goal or fulfilment just as did the folksong-like tune in the *prima parte* of the Third Quartet. After this the music threatens to break up in contrary-motion *glissandi* (as in the Third Quartet) and dramatic textural confrontations, and it is at this point that Bartók introduces what amounts to a recapitulation in the classical sense (bars 92–3).

Whether what precedes it is to the same extent classical seems more than doubtful. If a development section really begins at bar 49 (as Bartók, Kárpáti and others agree) it is hard to see in what way it influences the character of the music, which seems to advance in one energetic and at times violent sweep towards the crisis between bars 60 and 92. Development up to bar 60 is more or less continuous, and it resumes in the recapitulation, and again in the Finale, where the material is greatly expanded and rearranged in importance but follows a similar path towards the same goal. In the end the sense of return vies with the classical idea of resolution for domination of the Quartet's closing pages.

Bartók described these two movements as the outer shell of a work whose kernel is the slow third movement (he called the second and fourth movements the inner shell), and this shows how the idea of balanced movements which are in reality part of the same 'sphere' evolved from the interleaving recapitulations of the Third Quartet. It shows moreover that the process was conscious; and finally it shows, by implication, how the more artificial five-movement plan of the later work nevertheless gave Bartók a much freer rein to express a variety of ideas in sharply contrasted moods. The sublime character of the third movement, one of the most beautiful and moving conceptions in the whole quartet literature, springs directly from the need to give it a quality of stillness and contemplation which would confirm it as the centre or turning-point of the world of conflicting emotions expressed in the outer four movements. This is Eliot's 'enchainment of past and future' working in practice. Music by its nature, and Bartók's perhaps even more than most, pushes forward to its conclusion. To check this impulse, to pull it so to speak into a controlled orbital type of motion, Bartók imposes a concentric form in which, retrospectively at least, the listener feels that the beginning and end lie somehow at the centre of events. 'Only by the form, the pattern,' to quote *Burnt Norton* again, 'can words or music reach the stillness.' Bartók had already experimented with what came to be known as his night-music style in the piano suite *Out of Doors* (1926), and in his later works it was to be his most characteristic and powerful way of curbing the wilder excesses of his 'Allegro barbaro' manner.

The slow movement of the Fourth Quartet, cautiously marked *non troppo lento*, achieves stillness by harmonic as much as by rhythmic means. Of course, it has none of the driving impulse of the outer four movements; but there is nevertheless plenty of energy in the folk-instrumental embellishments of the cello and, later, violin melodies, and in their characteristic snapped rhythms. What gives the music its unique quality of suspension in space and time is the nearly motionless chordal accompaniment and above all its context. After two movements of swift motion and complicated chromatic textures, the placid diatonic opening chord spills downwards on to the cello solo like a splash of cool water. Thereafter it remains unaltered (a simple E major hexachord) until bar 13, where it changes to a slightly more complex inversion of a chord on A which is itself then held until, at bar 21, a linking chord introduces the third and most dissonant of the three main harmonies in the first section of the movement. The opening chord, as Kárpáti has shown, is a compressed form of a cycle of fifths on A; the final chord of the movement is the same, opened out (with an alien D natural added at the top). This is an essentially relaxed chord-formation; certainly its dissonances are mild compared with what our ears have grown accustomed to in the preceding movements. 'Tension grows', says Kárpáti, 'in proportion to the disintegration of the fifth-structure and the enrichment of the melodic elements.' In other words, each successive chord is slightly more dissonant and slightly less simple in its acoustical structure, and this corresponds to a marked intensification in the melody, and in the performance markings, leading eventually to *agitato* at the most complex point (bar 42) with a return to *tranquillo* at the more diatonic passage at bar 56, misleadingly described by Bartók as a free recapitulation, but perhaps better understood as a synthesis of the various ideas heard previously.

Although the harmonic role of these chords cannot be ignored, their most important and striking function is to provide an iridescent framework for the lovely cello melody, which unwinds in rhapsodic and rather melancholy fashion underneath. The romantic eloquence of this solo hardly needs emphasising; its tone derives a certain exotic strangeness from the typically Magyar chromatic displacements. What is perhaps not so obvious is the subtle relationship between it and the accompanying chords:

Ex.13   **Poco agitato** ♩ = 70

Evidently the chords are not in any traditional sense a 'harmonis-ation' of the melody. Instead they tend to complement it by supplying those notes of the octave which it does not contain. At bar 22, the third section, this relationship becomes absolutely pure: that is, while the chord contains six different notes, the melody contains the other six, and only those six (until bar 27). The dislocation between the two parts does to some extent help increase the tension; but this is reduced again by the fact that the relationship is for some time static and perhaps also by the fact that it constitutes, taken as a whole, a complete chromatic system. Several writers have drawn attention to the resemblance between this device and an aspect of twelve-note technique. Bartók never writes serially in the sense of sticking to a preordained *sequence* of notes, but he does occasionally (as here) deploy the twelve notes in a comprehensive and systematic way which closely resembles Berg's use of tropes (or non-ordered note-groups) in his serial music. Moreover, Bartók's music of this period has two other general features in common with Schoenbergian practice. First, it ignores the traditional structural differences between the horizontal (or melodic) dimension and the vertical (or harmonic). Thus in the slow movement of the Fourth Quartet the chords and melodies differ only in that in the one case the notes are heard simultaneously while in the other they are heard consecutively; the two are not governed by different rules, as are traditional melody and harmony, and their roles could easily be reversed. Secondly, every aspect of the music is motivic, including both the chordal and melodic elements, and also the rhythm.

For the best illustration of these points let us return to the opening of the work. Each of the distinct two- or three-bar cells which make up the first thirteen bars seems to present a different aspect of a single basic sculptural group, rather in the manner of a mobile whose components move constantly in relation to one another without damaging the integrity of the whole. Bartók's components are, for the most part, three-note scales, either chromatic or diatonic, and usually articulated by regular rhythmic patterns of quavers or semiquavers. In the first cell, which contains eleven of the twelve notes (all but A flat) and thus acts as a kind of matrix for later cells, the components are still indistinct – the three-note groups are intact but have not yet formed into scales. The scales crystallise in the third cell (bar 5 with its upbeat), in the form of a close chromatic canon from which there emerge, first, a cluster-like group whose texture will be a primary element of the whole movement, and, second, a pregnant chromatic motive built from two three-note scales (one rising, one falling) and picked out by the cello on its A string, fortissimo and with a hard semi-staccato attack:

Ex.14

This is the most important motive in the work. In its various guises it represents what one might call the most representative form of the work's motivic material (though several longer melodies evolve independently of it). It dominates all the crucial structural points of the first movement, especially the crisis before the recapitulation, the recap itself, and the coda, and it returns in the Finale to clinch the association of themes in the two movements and to end the Quartet with an exact replica of the end of the first movement.

But more generally the elements from which this motive itself emerged control every aspect of the first movement: its melody, its texture and harmony, and its rhythm. For instance, the cluster-textures which constantly threaten to disrupt the music's forward motion, and which have often been explained as a pianistic device borrowed perhaps from the American composer Henry Cowell, whom Bartók met in Paris in 1923, are actually thematic to the last degree and a true string-quartet effect derived from closely-woven melodic lines with or without chordal support. Similarly the rhythm is almost wholly based on the regular three-quaver group and its derivatives in the first and third cells of the movement.

A third characteristic of this movement seems to suggest the influence of Schoenberg: its remarkable dependence on elementary contrapuntal devices such as canon, imitation by direct or contrary motion, and symmetrical patterns based on those procedures. In fact Bartók's fondness for this type of symmetry amounts almost to an obsession; and his use of it is quite personal. In Schoenberg (if not in Webern) canon, fugue and imitation have their traditional aim of producing a texture which is at the same time highly unified and strongly directional; it moves forward, growing and developing as it goes, while sticking closely to a single generating idea. But in Bartók, such devices tend rather to check, even at times contradict, the music's forward progress. They are, it seems, the biggest single force opposing the sheer aggression and violent energy of what one might call the animal impulse. And in particular they control the movement's peculiar cell-structure. Notice, for instance, how the first rounded statement of the basic motive (bars 11–13) is completely governed by symmetries of one kind or another: its own near palindromic shape, the canon by retrograde-inversion in the second violin and cello (though the rhythm is not retrograded), followed by a canon by inversion, with a tiny canonic codetta all within the space of two bars:

Ex.15

This becomes a model for episode after episode: for example, the more elaborate handling of the same motive at bar 26, the multiple-stop *pesante* chords at 37, the more fluid chordal ostinato passage at 44, or, in Bartók's so-called 'development' section, the canon starting in bar 54, and the rich imitative treatment of the second (bar 14) theme at bars 59–60 etc., where the texture strongly resembles a passage early in the Third Quartet (see fig. 4, 'Più andante'). All these passages, incidentally, divide the instruments into balancing pairs.

The fact that the symmetries turn out on close examination to be for the most part slightly inexact in no way spoils their significance. If they were literal they would hardly intrigue the ear as they do, though they might be easier to analyse. As it is, the slight distortion of these neat and self-contained patterns is obviously an expression of the violent emotions at work in the music. Moreover it is crucial to the feeling of development and growth which remains fundamental to Bartók's thinking.

The same kind of rule governs the relationship between the balancing movements in the arch form. Again there is no question of literal architectural resemblance. On the contrary, the differences are as much a part of the scheme as are the similarities. In the Finale the components of the first movement, though still recognisable, are completely reorganised and the emphases redistributed. The first subject is now what was, in the first movement, the 'second theme' (bar 15, second violin, cf. Finale bar 15), while the second main subject (bar 156, first violin) is a fairly obvious, if more remote, derivative of the subsidiary syncopated theme at bar 40 of the first movement. On the other hand the principal chromatic material from the first movement, and in particular the basic motive first heard in the cello at bar 7, only begins to assert itself in the latter stages of the finale, and is not at all dominant until the final page, where it triumphantly – if darkly – clinches the whole scheme.

Bartók's choice of comparatively diatonic ideas from the first movement as principal material of the Finale is obviously not accidental. Both the fourth and fifth movements of the Quartet present what might be described as a more 'open' view of the themes from the second and first movements (respectively) on which they are based – as if the arch were being looked at not face on but at an angle, with one pillar nearer the eye than the other. Hence the curious mixture of spatial symmetry and temporal change which typifies this above all of Bartók's cyclic works.[1] One can see at a glance how the main Finale theme has an altogether more spaced-out character than it had in the first movement; its melodic intervals tend to be larger

---

[1] Ernö Lendvai has beautifully described these symmetrical forms of Bartók's as 'bridges' at whose centre a transformation takes place: darkness into light, or time into space. See Lendvai, 'Pizzicato Effect in Bartók's Fifth String Quartet', *New Hungarian Quarterly*, No.82. (Summer 1981), pp.84–90.

(see, for example, bar 31, where the chief interval is the perfect fourth), and the whole episode unfolds on a more generous time-scale, with long gaps between phrases of the theme during which the music consists solely of pounding chord patterns with a distinct peasant-dance flavour. Furthermore, Bartók makes little use here of the tight cell-variation technique or of the elaborate contrapuntal symmetries of the first movement. The music is in every way simpler and more extrovert, exuberant rather than aggressive, and it remains so to the end despite the clinching basic motive.

The result of this novel approach to the idea of tension-and-release is that the work's scheme of movement pairs turns out to be a good deal more complicated than the arch idea might suggest. True, the ABCBA scheme is paramount. But set against it we have a pattern in which the first two (chromatic) movements balance the last two (diatonic) ones, with the third movement – shifting subtly between the diatonic and the fully chromatic – as an arbiter between them. This plan is also held fast by thematic or at least textural links, and also by the tonal scheme. Like all Bartók's music of this period, the Fourth Quartet is tonal only in that it uses certain notes as points of reference; tonal logic in the classical sense is replaced by a largely motivic approach to chords and chord-progression. Bartók considered this quartet to be 'on' (rather than 'in') C, and the outer movements begin and end with that note prominent. By the same token the second movement is on E, a major third above C, while the fourth is on A flat, a major third below. So the relation between the last two movements, taken as a pair, repeats that between the first two. As for the thematic links, these are best seen in the light of the textural contrast between the two scherzo movements. The first, 'prestissimo con sordino', is largely based on scurrying triplet chromatic scale-figures, except for the trio section (bar 76 etc.), where the theme, a cell-like motive developed mainly by imitation, twists the chromatic lines inwards to a semiquaver rhythm taken from bar 5 of the first movement. The veiled, muted texture, which may have been suggested by the 'Allegro misterioso' of Berg's *Lyric Suite*, forms an immediate kinship with the compressed polyphony of the first movement, even though the Prestissimo has a freer, more regular movement and a much less rigorous motivic treatment. By contrast, the lighter and more attenuated pizzicato sound of Bartók's fourth movement, with its relaxed waltz tempo, anticipates the brilliant dance character of the Finale. This Allegretto pizzicato follows the outline of the earlier scherzo more closely than the Finale does that of the first movement. The main theme is like an opened-out version of the chromatic up-and-down scales in the Prestissimo (it now covers a full octave, in a typical Bartók diatonic scale with sharpened fourth and flattened seventh, instead of the chromatically-filled perfect fifth of the earlier movement), while the trio theme recurs with its original chromatic shape, its tensions much relieved, however, by the rippling pizzicato sound.

These two movements, with their vital contrast between sono-rities, lead us on to one of the most celebrated aspects of this great work: its exploration of new string-quartet sounds and invention of new string techniques. Bartók's model here was certainly the *Lyric Suite*, behind which stand in turn the earlier expressionist orchestral masterpieces of Berg himself, Schoenberg and Webern. No doubt Bartók was impressed by the variety of timbre and the virtuosity of treatment in Berg's quartet. But while he borrowed some of Berg's best effects (such as the scurrying *con sordino* and *sul ponticello* of the Allegro misterioso, or the sweeping *glissandi* of the Presto delirando), many of his ideas are new and seem to suggest the influence of folk-music as much as of expressionism. For instance, his love of massive and usually 'mistuned' multiple-stops, his invention of the snapped pizzicato (now widely known by his name) in which the string rebounds against the fingerboard, and his alternation (in the slow movement) of vibrato and non-vibrato chords – these may all be memories of the twanging, even harsh sound of peasant fiddling. Admittedly in this same movement he also uses a rapid alternation of *tremolo sul ponticello* and *tremolo ordinario* which seems to evoke the spectral imagery of expressionist instrumentation. But such writing in Bartók is often strictly thematic. In the first movement of the Fourth Quartet, for instance, the recurrent cluster-textures are, as we have seen, merely a consequence of the chromatic melodic lines working against each other, though the result sounds like an invention primarily of sonority. The same might also be said of the *glissandi* in this movement (a feature too of the Third Quartet). In general the Third and Fourth Quartets mark the appearance in Bartók's work of a structural approach to timbre, an increasing tendency which probably owes as much to French models as to German or Austrian.

By general agreement, the Fourth Quartet is the climax of Bartók's efforts to evolve an individual and comprehensive language through the medium of the string quartet, and to embody that language in an adequate architectural form. Here structural tension and mass are achieved without sacrifice of expressive range – indeed the immense contrast between the poetic slow movement and the grinding cerebration of the first movement is the work's most arresting feature, and a sure sign of Bartók's confidence in his mastery of the genre. In achieving it Bartók seems at the same time to have lifted himself out of the stylistic impasse which the Violin Sonatas, the First Piano Concerto and the Third Quartet might have represented. Lyricism and freshness flow back into his next group of works, to the extent that the Fifth Quartet, though it resembles the Fourth in design, belongs in reality to a new phase of his music. If the Fourth is in this sense a transitional work, the transition is one which shows the very essence of Bartók's style and nature, and while the later quartets are hardly less brilliant in execution or rich in expression the Fourth remains unique in its uncompromisingly dangerous, but eventually truthful and satisfying reconciliation of extreme expressive opposites.

String Quartet No. 5

Just as the differences between the Third and Fourth Quartets can be exaggerated through a comparison of their structure, so the differences between the Fourth and Fifth are sometimes underrated for the same reason. In the Fifth, Bartók again adopts an arch-form of five movements. And since the Second Piano Concerto, one of only two large-scale works Bartók wrote in between, has the same basic scheme (disguised as the traditional three concerto movements), the temptation to group this series of works is obvious. Nevertheless the stylistic differences are striking. One has only to compare the pure G major trumpet tune which starts the Concerto with even the relatively 'open' material in the last two movements of the Fourth Quartet to notice this change. Admittedly the question of medium has to be taken into account. The concerto first movement is written for piano and wind, an irreproachably clean-cut combination, and in the Fifth Quartet there is some return to the more densely woven textures of the Fourth. But the treatment of the ideas, and even of the form, is in many respects new. The cell method plays very little part in the Fifth, and in its place we find once again extended melodic periods and formal contrasts arising, as in classical music, out of something other than a ruthlessly logical continuity. This is as yet a somewhat theoretical classicism, and the music's immediate impact is every bit as aggressive, if not quite so abrasive, as that of the Fourth. It is hard to account for the contemporary Hungarian critic Sándor Jemnitz finding in the Fifth Quartet 'the calm ease of classic sages', except as a response to its technical mastery, which is certainly prodigious.

In the period between the completion of the Fourth Quartet in September 1928 and the composition of the Fifth in August and September 1934 (to a commission by Elisabeth Sprague Coolidge), Bartók was once again preoccupied with folk music. This is the time of the folksong-based violin duos (1931) and the first extensive work on the graded piano pieces of *Mikrokosmos*, which erect a keyboard method on simple folk-like tunes and rhythms. Bartók also made orchestral transcriptions of certain earlier folk-music works, as well as some new arrangements for solo voice or chorus (grouped round the big choral masterpiece of 1930, the *Cantata Profana*). It seems obvious that this return to his musical roots was a subconscious part of his emergence from the enclosed and tortuous world of the previous two quartets. The Fourth Quartet had, so to speak, opened the door, and now Bartók at last steps outside, takes a deep breath and looks around him. Compare the elliptical, claustrophobic opening phrase of the Fourth Quartet (two *allegro* bars, including a final crotchet rest) with the broad expanse of the Fifth Quartet's initial theme, which covers thirteen bars of common time. Yet the difference is due not to any rejection of the chromaticism of the earlier work, but to a willingness to ventilate that chromaticism, one might almost say to dramatise it, through repetition, a rhetorical unison texture, and powerful rhythmic gestures. This is admittedly an extreme example of the contrast between the two works. There are passages in the Fourth Quartet, including the first movement, where repetition is important and where the rhythmic gestures are bold; and there are a few episodes in the Fifth where the weaving of four chromatic lines produces an effect almost as opaque as the most characteristic multiple-stopped canonic cell in the Fourth. But there is no accumulation of such episodes. And it must be said that in the Fourth Quartet repetition usually takes the form of ostinato, a relatively artificial extension device, whereas in the Fifth (though ostinato is used here too) it more often belongs to the structural and polyphonic expansion and development of the themes.

Because the themes in the Fifth Quartet open out into periods which, in general type at least, resemble those of classical music more closely than they do the tight variation-cells of the Fourth, its whole design has a more open and generous feeling. In the first movement a sonata kind of pattern, with contrasted subject groups, is plain to see, though Bartók typically rearranges its components into something like an arch form. The muscular first subject, with its obsessive hammering-out of the tonic-centre B flat and its 'mistuned' dominant E, is soon followed by a quiet *leggiero* bridge passage in free canon which resolves, by way of a novel but unmistakable sequence of leading harmonies, into a second subject in a Bartókian C minor, marked by energetic cross-rhythms (bar 25). After this Bartók makes a brief reference to the opening theme, and then launches at bar 44 into a flowing third subject apparently in B flat but cadencing conventionally on the true dominant of that key (F) at what is obviously the end of the exposition, bar 58. The significant point about this exposition is that each of its five sections (counting the two bridge passages) makes a comprehensive textural, tonal and rhythmic contrast with its neighbours, so that despite the usual motivic links the listener gets something of that sense of diverse formal elements so characteristic of the classical sonata exposition. In the development these elements are juxtaposed more freely, and their relationships discussed, still with an expansive, almost flamboyant, freedom utterly different from the abrupt head-on collisions in the corresponding part of the Fourth Quartet. The recapitulation then fulfils its traditional function of restating the original thematic groups in such a way that they confirm and strengthen the tonic key.

From this somewhat bald description it might well appear that Bartók wrote the Fifth Quartet in some spirit of recantation: that the work is a deliberate reaffirmation of classical principles. But this is true only in the most general sense. Bartók is certainly concerned here with formal balance, with a clear-cut relationship between the parts and the whole. But so he was in all his earlier quartets. If, seen from a certain distance, the first movement of the Fifth Quartet looks rather like sonata form (as did the first movement of the Second), the same could be said of the Fourth Quartet – if we are to believe Bartók himself, not to mention the ultramodern and by no means sycophantic Kárpáti. It simply depends how far away you stand. But if we move in close and examine the Fifth in more detail, something rather different appears.

The large form of the Quartet is an arch, similar to that of the Fourth Quartet. The outer movements correspond in certain ways (including the cyclic recurrence of some, but not all, of their themes), the even-numbered movements balance one another similarly, and the whole structure pivots on a central movement which has special qualities to fit it for that role. In the Fifth this central movement is a dance scherzo, and the even-numbered movements which frame it are slow (a reversal of the plan in the Fourth). The special 'fitting' property of the scherzo is that it is itself an arch, that is ternary, form with, at its heart, a basically very simple folksong episode rendered subtle by incredible virtuosity of rhythm and sonority, just as the slow movement of the Fourth was a basically simple folktune rendered subtle by linear and harmonic embellishment. We have seen that the first movement is also in some sense an arch. Not only are the themes reversed in the recapitulation, but they are inverted, in the Schoenbergian sense. But that this is a structural, rather than a merely thematic, inversion is shown – as Milton Babbitt has pointed out – by the fact that in turning his themes upside down Bartók effectively inverts the whole score.[1] It begins to appear at this point that mirror-images of one kind or another may run deep into the fabric of the whole Quartet.

Symmetry and contrapuntal ingenuity played a large role in the Fourth Quartet, as part of an unprecedented motivic saturation of the music. In the Fifth Quartet, where the motivic element is less overpowering, symmetries pervade every aspect of the argument – one could almost say of the musical language, since Bartók resolutely employs scales and harmonies with symmetrical properties. The central illustration of this is his preference for the mistuned (flattened) dominant, which divides the octave in two equal halves and therefore lends itself to exact melodic imitations within a fixed tonal framework. In view of the importance Bartók attaches in this work to exact mirror imitations, the equal division of the octave is virtually an automatic mechanism of his desire for formal stability. A simple illustration is provided by the last three bars of the work, where Bartók cadences on a (carefully delayed) B flat from a unison E, by way of contrary-motion scales that exactly invert one another:

[1] Milton Babbitt, 'The String Quartets of Bartók', *Musical Quarterly*, XXXV (1949), p.383.

Ex.16

But the mechanical aspect of this technique is hardly a sufficient description, though it may be part of one. Modern Hungarian criticism has put forward a number of (mutually contradictory) explanations of Bartók's obsession with the tritone: Lendvai will tell us that it comes from an axial interpretation of the circle of fifths in which the four cardinal points of each axis are all tonally equivalent (so in B flat, the notes C sharp, E and G are substitute *tonics*); Kárpáti will say, with some authority from Bartók himself, that on the contrary E is the mistuned *dominant* of B flat; various ethnomusicologists will point to the prevalence of the sharpened fourth in Arab and Rumanian folk music, which Bartók collected and studied. The truth is that, while all these explanations may fit selected cases, none of them fits every case – for the good reason that Bartók's attraction to the tritone lay in its combination of opposed qualities. On the one hand it was a stable element, connected with equal divisions, axes, and suchlike rather geometrical concepts. On the other it was the tensest of all intervals, *diabolus in musica*, deriving its nature from its very disobedience to acoustic laws of precedence. The former property satisfied his constructivist tendencies; the latter his urge for expression. He thus equivocated between different acoustic principles, and no explanation of his use of the tritone – at least in his later works – is adequate unless it allows for this double function.

The start of the Fifth Quartet offers a striking illustration. In between the hammered B flats, Bartók gradually constructs a scale: C, then after a time D flat, then D natural, E flat and, heavily emphasised, E natural. This is not a simple chromatic scale. The D flat and natural, separated by the root B flat, are the minor and major third in conflict, the E flat is the fourth of either scale, and we expect F as its conventional fifth. The E natural thus creates a momentary clash in the listeners' mind; and although Bartók continues the melody (see unison viola and cello in bar 5 etc.) without reference to that clash, by oscillating between E and its regular tonic A, he keeps up the expressive tension by bringing in the hammered B flats at precisely this moment in the upper parts. So on the one hand we have two complementary 'systems', one on B flat, one on its opposite pole E (to use Lendvai terminology); on the other we have a violent and persistent semitonal clash, between E and the implied F, and between A and B flat (very much stated). Bartók was evidently excited by this clash for its own sake, and it quickly becomes a feature of the part writing. Notice the deliberately timed examples in bar 8 (D/D flat, and F against the stressed violin E), and the large number of semitonal dissonances in the pseudo-canonic bridge passage which follows. If we compare the viola entry in bar 14 with the first violin's imitation of this entry in the next bar, we can see that Bartók actually changes the figure to ensure that there is a semitone (or to be precise a major seventh) clash on the final note each time:

Ex.17

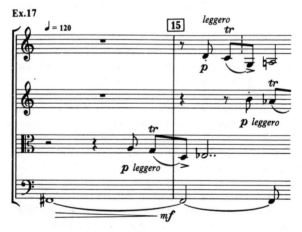

The expressive meaning of such a device naturally depends on the context. In the Fourth Quartet semitonal dissonance generally contains some direct reference to the semitone-based thematic material. But in the Fifth there is something more concrete about the treatment, as if the semitones were consciously there to disrupt the confident and self-satisfied unisons which abound in this work. The first E natural is a pointed and even brutal dislocation of the B flat material. But the dislocation is not always so violent. In the bridge passage there is something almost wry about the 'misplaced' notes, and in the calm C major episode of the first slow movement (Adagio molto, bar 10) Bartók achieves an indescribable piquancy of effect by presenting the violin melody on D flat rather than C. This is one of the crucial passages in the whole Quartet, seeming to reach to the heart of the modern composer's hopeless yearning for a simple but searching expressive language to match the pure eloquence of Mozartian classicism. At the climax of the work, when the Finale seems to be rushing to its close, Bartók suddenly refers back to this calm moment in an extraordinary, parenthetic episode which he marks, with untypical theatricality, 'Allegretto, con indifferenza' (bar 699). The rising theme from the Adagio (which is also virtually the main theme of the Finale in inversion) appears now in a completely diatonic A major, in the guise of a cheap hurdy-gurdy tune with a *meccanico* Alberti bass. But after one statement of the tune, it starts again a semitone higher, still against A major harmonies, exactly reproducing the relationship in the C major Adagio passage except that here the semitone dislocation is insisted on mechanically, whereas in the Adagio it was soon resolved (Ex. 18 overleaf).

This is one of the few episodes in Bartók which invite verbal explanation – indeed it seems positively to crave it. And in this the composer's grip, normally so firm and masterful, perhaps for once slackens. For the mockery of the 'con indifferenza' is directed, of course, not against popular music, or Mozart, or the Romantics (all of which have been suggested), but against himself, against his own secret fear of cheapness and emotional triviality. Is it not the case, the music seems to ask, that all these violent discordant strivings and elaborate intellectualisations are merely self-advertising histrionics? Is such an emotional exhibition to be tolerated in this day and age? A cheap melody is after all a cheap melody, in or out of tune. As already noted, Bartók had a certain distaste for baring his soul. He suffered, like T. S. Eliot in Edmund Wilson's description, 'the peculiar conflicts of the Puritan turned artist'. We may even hear in this music Eliot's street piano, 'mechanical and tired . . . Recalling things that other people have desired'. But Bartók cannot disown the desire so readily. It is his own, as the music makes unmistakably clear.

Ex.18

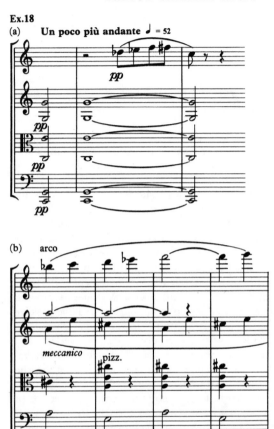

The theme itself has already dominated the Finale, with a typically Bartókian mixture of sheer physical exuberance and thoroughgoing economy of organisation. The long first-subject group (bars 14–149) is derived almost exclusively from various polyphonic combinations of the brusque five-note descending figure played in unison by the top three instruments after letter A (Ex. 19a), and this, as can be best seen by examining the rising form at letter B, is simply the Adagio and 'con indifferenza' theme with the fifth diminished to a tritone (Ex. 19b). The opening statement is the clearest illustration in the work of Kárpáti's dominant-function E in the key of B flat.

Ex.19

(a)

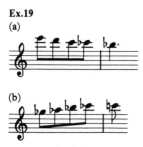

(b)

But even here Bartók is playing on the minor second clash as well
(the first note after letter A is an F), and the whole section is
marvellously rich in semitonal feints both because of the tritone and
because Bartók characteristically uses different forms of his scale
according to whether it is rising or falling, so that for instance in the
melody of bars 18–20 there is a constant and rapid equivocation
between C natural and C flat as the line arches up and down. Such
points perhaps counterbalance any mechanical or schematic tendency in the network of exact imitations, inversions and retrogrades
which forms the basis of this section. But Bartók also varies the
texture with enormous dexterity. He switches deftly from two-part
counterpoint with the instruments paired (as often in the Fourth
Quartet), to flowing patterns of four-part fugato and stretto and
contrary-motion passages of varying density, then back to simple
melody with an ostinato rhythmic accompaniment. After a bridge
passage where he toys with a mechanical scheme of chords radiating
from a common axis, he picks up the last of these chords (the major
seventh F sharp/G) and turns it into a melody which he then
proceeds also to treat by canonic imitation in tandem with a rising
and falling melody which plainly echoes the first subject but with its
tritones smoothed out into perfect fourths. This second subject
group (bars 202–348 – for some reason Ligeti, in his analysis printed
in the Philharmonia miniature score, calls it a 'Trio') forms a variety
of imitative textures hardly less patterned than that of the first. At bar
224 the rising-falling theme is worked into a rigid double canon by
inversion. But the tone of the whole section is different because the
tritone is absent, as too is the stressed semitone (after the first
flourishes of the major-seventh theme). Both are restored, however,
in the fugue which forms the central section of the movement, and
which in many ways recalls the clinching fugue in the development

of the *seconda parte* in the Third Quartet. The theme, rather unexpectedly, is the first subject of the first movement, and Bartók now sets the seal on its tritone character by bringing in his entries alternately on E and B flat (instead of the conventional tonic-dominant) and marking the rhythm with drum-like tritone chords, played *col legno*. Appended to this is a set of entries outlining what Lendvai would call the subdominant axis (C – A – F sharp), dissolving in a final inverted entry on the tonic E (cello, bar 420).

It would be possible to continue this account of the music's polyphonic complexities on through the recapitulation and even ironically enough beyond the deprecating 'con indifferenza' episode. Yet the movement hardly feels like an intellectual construction, and it would be wrong to see its systematic elements as the creative essence of the music. Rather, as we saw in the Third and Fourth Quartets, they channel and direct that essence in various ways which still strike one as representing Bartók the sentient being as well as Bartók the scheming mind.

This genius for combining supreme creative energy with a systematic organisation of his material is apparent in the more straightforward central movements of the Fifth Quartet as well as the complex outer ones. In the scherzo *alla bulgarese* it can even be seen as an agent of simplicity, like the organisation of very simple children's songs or folksongs in which a few elementary phrases are repeated, perhaps at different pitches, to make up the whole tune. The main theme is largely constructed from strings of thirds, alternating major and minor in such a way (Kárpáti has shown) as to imply a cycle of interleaved perfect fifths: (Ex. 20).

Ex.20

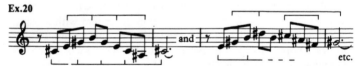

The curious 9/8 rhythm (4+2+3) is also treated quite mechanically. Each bar repeats the same pattern until the arresting change at letter A, where the smooth quavers are temporarily disrupted by a more dance-like melody which makes more of a point of the unequal division of the bar. And in the astonishing trio section, one of the most original and fascinating pieces in the whole quartet literature, the element of repetition is carried to an extreme. The whirling ostinatos undergo only slight and barely perceptible modification as they slowly climb in pitch; and how typical that Bartók, wishing to elaborate the texture slightly, should do so by adding an exact inversion of the violin figure (bar 42). Yet the melody itself – another gently stylised folk tune with a subtle choriambic arrangement of dotted crotchets and crotchets – is as fresh as if Bartók had just discovered it in the Mátra and simply adapted it to the alien Bulgarian rhythm.

As for the balancing slow movements, their similarities of form are not quite so far-reaching as those of the equivalent scherzos in the Fourth Quartet, nor are they as intense in feeling as that work's great Adagio, though the Andante of the Fifth Quartet rises eventually to a powerful, somewhat rhetorical climax. Bartók is content merely to hint at certain elements of reprise in this movement. Thus the nebulous introductory music, with its weird pizzicato *glissandi* and repeated notes played on alternate open and stopped strings (one wonders whether Bartók hoped for slight fluctuations of pitch as well as timbre from this effect), is obviously an expanded form of the even more wraith-like music which opens the Adagio molto. Similarly the chordal figuration at letter A of each movement is parallel from a structural point of view, though its effect is completely changed by the staccato repetitions in the Andante, and the important rising melody of the Adagio is nowhere to be found. But from letter B in the Andante Bartók embarks on a richly embroidered development of the next group of themes from the Adagio which goes far beyond the somewhat hesitant character of that original material and brings it to a melodic climax of such weight that it almost completely obliterates the arch form so clear in the earlier movement. It almost seems that Bartók may have overridden his own first intentions here. The reprise of the slow chords at letter D (now smooth again, as in the Adagio) is still scattered with debris from the eruption just past; the reference to the staccato chords (at bar 95) is a mere apology; and the introductory music is not reprised at all, unless we count the strange, triple-stopped pizzicato *glissandi* on the cello as a kind of instant fusion of all the elements in that section.

Thus Bartók's expressive instincts refuse to allow him to be dominated by a constructivist idea. Nevertheless the relation between these two movements is a good deal more explicit than the fragmentary and rather amorphous connections between the outer movements of the Second Quartet, or between the *prima parte* and its 'recapitulation' in the Third. In these later works Bartók's use of the cyclic principle is decidedly more solid than before. But it is not inert, and it retains much that is unpredictable and intuitive – much of that capriciousness of detail without which symmetry in art is a mere empty show.

Sonata for Two Pianos and Percussion

In the very month in which he completed the Fifth Quartet, Bartók finally abandoned his teaching work at the Academy of Music in Budapest. He had been commissioned by the Hungarian Academy of Sciences to make a systematic classification of his folk music collection, and this work was to occupy a large part of his time until he left Budapest for good in October 1940. But though the work, with its more private character, was certainly more congenial to Bartók than teaching, he was not to be spared the frustration inseparable from artistic life in an increasingly politicised state. His music became an object of attack in the right-wing press (as expressing 'a bleak, destructive soul') and the Singing Youth movement, with which both Bartók and Kodály had been closely associated, was more and more a battleground for extreme political ideologies to which neither composer subscribed. Bartók himself can scarcely have been surprised at these tendencies. By 1937, when his Aryanism was investigated by the German Reichs-Musikkammer, he was well aware of the threat posed by Nazism to free artistic expression in a country such as Hungary, which already had an entrenched proto-Fascist regime. For years his music had been regarded with suspicion by the Budapest musical establishment. Incredibly, not a single major work of his after the Fourth Quartet had its first performance in Hungary; the *Cantata Profana*, completed in 1930 and first heard in London in 1934, was not performed in Budapest until 1936.

The shadow cast by these circumstances, though it falls on Bartók's correspondence of the mid-1930s and later, takes longer to reach his music. The two great masterpieces of 1936–7, the *Music for strings, percussion and celesta* and the *Sonata for two pianos and percussion*, exude an almost Olympian spirit of emotional freedom and detachment, a quality for which Bartók had fought too hard to allow himself to be cheated of it by material considerations. The 'bleak, destructive soul' seems as far from this music as 'the unyielding cries of men who are prepared to die for the cause of freedom' (to quote Ujfallussy's statement of an interpretation favoured, perhaps not surprisingly, by modern Hungarian criticism).

Instead it is the spirit of gaiety, in the most positive sense, which predominates. More than any of Bartók's larger compositions, these are works which dance, and they do so in a pure, if somewhat hard, sunlight. The aggressive violence of earlier dance works such as *The Miraculous Mandarin*, and the earthy exuberance of movements inspired, like the scherzo of the Second Quartet or the Allegro moderato of the Piano Sonata, by peasant dance, are now transfigured into a controlled but magnificently vital energy expressed in a brilliant play of movement and colour.

This shift of emphasis is already implicit in Bartók's choice of instruments for the two works. They pursue a line taken from the piano works of 1926 (including the First Concerto), through the Second Concerto of 1931, and to a large extent side-stepping the febrile contrapuntal insistence of the string quartets. Clearly there are dense contrapuntal episodes, especially in the *Music for Strings*, but they now serve as only one textural element among many forming the complete structured vocabulary of the work. Moreover they are more schematic even than in the Fifth Quartet, and not nearly so volatile. Above all, Bartók's concern in this series of works seems to be for coherent and lucid architecture, articulated through timbre and rhythm as much as motive. He had been a pioneer of the percussive treatment of the piano, but more recently he had experimented with a hard, crystalline piano sound offset by variable orchestral groupings and extended by other percussion instruments treated somewhat in the manner of a one-man band. The Second Concerto already shows a rather sophisticated handling of this idea, with the piano set against distinct orchestral family groups and occasionally joined by percussion soloists to make a kind of skeletal concerto grosso. In the *Music for Strings* the treatment is even more subtle, and uses the whole spectrum of sound, from unpitched percussion, through clear, immobile pitch of piano, xylophone and celesta, up to the flexible pitch and sonority of the string orchestra, to outline the entire form of the work. The *Sonata* refines and specialises this treatment, translating it into a new species of chamber music and limiting it to one end of the tonal spectrum.

Like the *Music for Strings* (which was commissioned by Paul Sacher for the Basle Chamber Orchestra) the *Sonata* was the result of a commission from Basle, this time from the local ISCM group, who wanted a chamber work to mark their tenth anniversary in January 1938. One supposes that they may have had in mind a new string quartet. But this seems to have been far from Bartók's mind. 'For some years now,' he wrote in the *Basler National Zeitung*, 'I have been planning to compose a work for piano and percussion. Slowly, however, I have become convinced that one piano does not sufficiently balance the frequently very sharp sounds of the percussion.' Thus there emerged the idea of a 'Quartet' written solely for percussion instruments, two of which, however, assume preeminence through their greater power and versatility. Although this idea is a logical enough extension of the concertante piano-and-percussion parts in the preceding works with orchestra, it seems to have caused anxiety to his publishers, as works in unfamiliar genres are apt to do, and it was at the instigation of Ralph Hawkes that Bartók rearranged the *Sonata for two pianos and percussion* as a concerto for two pianos and orchestra late in 1940. However, the transcription must be regarded as a dilution of the original work, and only a very doubtful alternative to it.

As chamber music, in the broadest sense of the term, the *Sonata* is unique. Here there is no attempt at those qualities of intimacy or profound psychological – intellectual investigation which had traditionally been the stuff of the greatest chamber works, from Haydn to Bartók himself. Instead the reduction of instruments is the refinement of a set idea. It enables elements of timbre to be isolated and particularised to the point where they become formative elements of quite unexpected power; it brings rhythm sharply into focus as a thematic as well as locomotive process; and it lends the harmony a certain diamantine objectivity which suits the less fluid motivic conception of the work. Nor does Bartók trouble to give the various performers the sort of equality they might have enjoyed in some theoretical high-classical quartet for these forces. Clearly he never thought in such terms at all. Just as the two pianos arose initially from the inadequacy of one, so Bartók was till quite a late stage uncertain (and apparently unconcerned) as to the number of players needed for the percussion part he had already composed. The score even allows the xylophone part to be taken, at need, by a third percussionist. The essential point is that the percussion part, as a whole, is a distinct organism formed out of a fairly small number of individual but related components and expressly designed to complement the pianos. Each of these percussion instruments has a strong character of its own; but this character, like that of a machine component, is too specialised to give the instrument much independence. Instead its role is to complement, emphasise, particularise, define or dramatise something being played or about to be played by the pianos. Thus the opening timpani roll, the cymbal clashes at bars 6 and 10 or the xylophone solo at bar 45 of the second movement, mainly serve to throw crucial points of the piano music into high relief. At times a percussion instrument may assume brief independence, like the alternately snared and unsnared side-drum taps from bar 41 of the first movement (a rhythmic abstract of the main theme), or the xylophone in the main theme of the Finale, whose purpose is to illuminate still more than a piano could the sudden diatonic clarity of that theme. Bartók invariably treats such passages not as extra noise, but as clarification. The dry-sounding percussion is used with astonishing delicacy amounting at times almost to a needle-point sensuality, a kind of aural tickle; and most of the score directions command restraint: for example, the final one tells the cymbalist to play 'with the fingernail, or the blade of a pocket-knife, on the very edge' (of the instrument). The heavier and more sonorous instruments are used more sparingly, apart from the timpani, which have to be the pedal type, and have a crucial role in defining the area between the unpitched drums and the pianos.

Bartók's concern in this work for aural spacing is balanced, as it is in the *Music for Strings*, by exact instructions about the physical placing of the various instruments. He even appends a map, showing the pianos on either side with their keyboards towards the audience, and the percussion grouped behind and between with the pitched instruments (xylophone and timpani) nearest to the pianos. In this way the percussion bodily fills the space between the pianos, as if it were no more than an extension backwards of the two instruments towards their vanishing point.

It is tempting to suggest that this 'three-dimensional' factor in the *Sonata* as he had already vaguely conceived it was what really led Bartók to bring in a second piano, so that the music would acquire a frame and a perspective. Certainly his treatment of the two pianos themselves is in general so similar that we often seem to be concerned simply with different views of the same object – a kind of parallactic shift in space and time. Canons and mirror canons abound between the two instruments; and while they were also indeed a feature of the Fifth Quartet, and while one often observes in Bartók's quartet-writing a curious two and two division of the score which gives it something of the look of certain pages in the Sonata (Ex. 21), nevertheless this division is in the nature of things much more marked and persistent in the piano work. Bartók nearly always treats the two hands as a unity; a remarkable proportion of the writing for each instrument is either unison or in parallel chords, or occasionally forms ostinatos by interwoven contrary-motion figures, as for

Ex.21
(a) String Quartet No.4

(b) Sonata for 2 pianos and percussion

instance in the first piano on page 11, where the two alternating chords pivot around the harmonically fixed element B-A flat, or (to take a more extreme case) in the ostinato passage which follows the fugal recapitulation of the third subject (bar 383 etc.), where the gigue-like accompanying figures form sequences of major thirds into complementary whole-tone scales making a complete twelve-note set (Ex. 22 overleaf). (Bartók had done something similar in his First Violin Sonata.

Ex.22 (Percussion omitted)

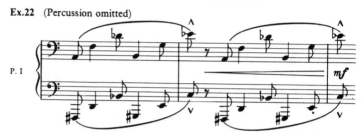

P. I

This kind of writing is fundamentally different from the traditional two-hand division into melody and harmony. It shows something of the shape and colour of Debussy's writing for two pianos in *En blanc et noir*. But the phasing of the two instruments in passages like the canonic Introduction or the (again canonic) extension of the third subject from bar 134, or the contrary-motion passage at bar 115 in the Finale, is a good deal more systematic than anything in Debussy and gives textures of much greater vigour and energy and movement than one finds even in that spirited piano-duo masterpiece.

The question of system in Bartók's *Sonata* has in fact been very much worked over, particularly in Hungarian writing on the master. Although the large-form generally follows the Fifth Quartet and the *Music for Strings* in reverting to fairly conventional sonata-type divisions, and even abandons the Fifth Quartet's arch-plan of movements, there seems little doubt that this innocent exterior conceals an inner scheme of thematic, harmonic, rhythmic and structural relationships of a density and richness unparalleled in the work of any earlier composer, with the possible exception of Berg who was of all the Viennese serialists the composer closest in temperament to Bartók.

The best and most original writer on this topic is the Budapest musicologist Ernö Lendvai, some of whose analyses have fortunately been published in English. Briefly, Lendvai's theory is that Bartók evolved a harmonic method based on an axial interpretation of the cycle of fifths, according to which all notes separated by a tritone or a minor third are equivalent in tonal function: for example, in the key of C, the notes E flat, F sharp and A may all act as substitute tonics; G, B flat, C sharp and E may all act as dominants; and F, A flat, B and D may all act as subdominants. Lendvai also considers that Bartók used the so-called Golden Section (the ratio ·618 . . . :1) both as a formal principle and as a regulator for harmonic and melodic intervals (by way of the Fibonacci series – 2, 3, 5, 8, 13, 21, 34 etc. – whose ratios gradually approach the true Golden Section). In the *Sonata* Lendvai shows impressive evidence for the structural use of the Golden Section. He finds a high incidence of significant event governed by the GS ratio in terms of bar-numbers or equal beats. For instance it turns out that the positioning of the entries in bars 2, 8 and 12 of the first movement is fixed by a GS count (though Lendvai has to ignore a crotchet rest in bar 8 to make the calculation work). On the larger scale the discovery that the first movement lasts precisely ·618 of the whole work (in terms of quaver beats) goes a long way towards proving that Bartók worked these ratios out consciously, particularly if one questions (as I do) Lendvai's argument that changes in the time value of the quaver pulse have no effect on the arithmetical value of the ratio.

As so far published in English at least, Lendvai's axis theory and his theory of Bartók's use of Fibonacci numbers to construct melodies and chords provide a valuable etymology for the composer's usage, but as chord grammar in the old sense they are still decidely primitive and as harmonic syntax – as an explanation, that is, of how Bartók's harmonies relate to the development of ideas and form – they hardly amount to a method at all. What they do is codify certain perhaps puzzling relationships and reference points which keep cropping up. For instance, they tell us why Bartók wrote the movements of his *Music for Strings* in, respectively, A, C, F sharp and A (with climaxes in E flat, F sharp, C and E flat); or why the first movement of the *Sonata* starts in F sharp though the key is C; or why melodies like the first theme in the *Sonata*'s second movement, or the xylophone tune at bar 48 of that movement, seem to rotate on axes of the Lendvai type. In fact they draw attention to a certain persistent melodic and harmonic colouring in Bartók's music of this period, derived from his preference for the tritone and minor third rather than the perfect fifth and major third of traditional tonal harmony. This is what gives the first two movements of the *Sonata* that crabbed, sideslipping quality which seems to us so peculiarly and piquantly Bartókian. It also lends the music its somethat muffled resonance, by denying the natural overtone responses on which the piano depends for that characteristic bloom we associate with Romantic keyboard music. Lendvai points out that the colour changes dramatically in the Finale, which is based on traditional primary chords and a melody of a frankly tonic-dominant cut. A certain feeling of harmonic *in*completeness dominates the early movements of the *Music for Strings* and the *Sonata for two pianos and percussion*; in both works 'completion' or 'resolution' is reserved for a diatonic finale.

Nevertheless the individual movements of the *Sonata* are perfectly self-contained and no longer display the far-reaching cyclic character of the quartets. The first movement is a fairly straightforward sonata form with three contrasted subjects (bars 32, 84 and 105 respectively) of which the second is recapitulated in inversion, as in the first movement of the Fifth Quartet, while the third returns as a fugato (bar 332). All this is prefaced by a brief but thematically and emotionally substantial introduction, a vestigial memory, perhaps, of the similar but far more elaborate slow fugue which had opened the *Music for Strings*. The mood is at first dark and forbidding. But even in the introduction it lacks the enervating intensity and sheer abrasiveness of so much earlier Bartók. And in the Allegro, though Bartók keeps us on edge with his harmonic equivocations, the vigorous nine-eight pulse (handled with a dazzling variety of subdivision) and the generous allowance of simple triads (mostly though not always in first inversion) give the music a vitality and radiance hardly to be found in Bartók's earlier music, for all its exuberant energy.

The other two movements together last about as long as the first. The night-music Lento makes some use of Debussian piano scales (though comparatively sparing use of the Debussian sustaining pedal), but in form most resembles the second slow movement of Bartók's Fifth Quartet, with a rather fragmentary reprise of the main thematic elements from earlier in the movement. After the subtleties of this music, the crude C major of the rondo Finale makes a positively blaring effect, though this is no more than an introductory gesture and is soon modified, first by the curious inflections (F sharp and B flat) of the xylophone tune and then by the more chromatic and elusive continuation of this theme at bar 28. Even so the diatonic feel of the movement is exceptionally strong, and it shows how completely Bartók has returned, admittedly on his own terms, to the concept of 'tonal music'. Even here parallel triads persistently weaken the functional workings of the harmony. But it is typical of Bartók, and especially of the *Sonata*, that it ends with a delicate joke at the expense of this very trait, with contrary-motion piano triads converging in the most oblique fashion on a not-quite-perfect C major cadence, accompanied by the sardonic clicking of the snared side-drum.

Bartók appended to the score the date-mark 'Budapest, 1937, VII–VIII'. But it appears that the work was already sketched in June, while he was holidaying in Carinthia; and moreover we gather from a letter of 2 September that at that stage the Finale was still no more than half-finished.[1] This warns us to be wary of Bartók's date-marks in general, as we have to be of the detailed timings which he entered in the majority of his scores after 1930; at any rate we should not take them too literally. The *Sonata* was first performed, on schedule, at the Basle anniversary concert of 16 January 1938, with Bartók and his second wife Ditta playing the piano parts. This was the first of many performances the couple gave of the *Sonata*, with various percussionists, including the Budapest première in October 1938. But by then the Austrian Anschluss had set in motion a train of events which would ensure that no such music was heard in central Europe for another seven years, by which time Bartók would be dying in another continent.

Contrasts and String Quartet No. 6

Some time after the Basle première of the *Sonata for two pianos and percussion* Bartók received another and more specific commission for a chamber work. The American jazz clarinettist Benny Goodman asked him for a short piece for clarinet, violin and piano which he and the violinist József Szigeti (who seems to have suggested the commission) could record on the two sides of a 78 rpm record. Even the character of the piece was stipulated. Goodman wanted something along the lines of Bartók's two-part Rhapsodies with their *lassú-friss* arrangement of movements. Such commissions were very much part and parcel of American musical life, with its increasing domination by the mechanical technology of the cinema and the gramophone. But Bartók was hardly used to working within limits of this kind, and it is not surprising that the finished work, which he eventually christened *Contrasts*, is both freer in style and a

[1] See J. Ujfalussy, *Béla Bartók* (English version, Budapest, 1971), p.321. No source is given for the information.

good deal longer than Goodman hoped. It seems that Bartók first composed the movements requested, probably in August 1938 (these are the outer movements of the eventual *Contrasts*), and they were played by Szigeti, Goodman and Endre Petri at Carnegie Hall in January 1939 under the title *Two Dances*. Together they last about eleven and a half minutes, against Goodman's proposed 'six to seven minutes'. And clearly the very extent of these pieces, which gives the opening *verbunkos* the character of an independent Allegro moderato rather than a slow rhapsodic introduction, decided Bartók that a central slow movement was needed to complete the form. He had indeed already composed this by the end of September 1938, though he only told Szigeti about it in December. The performance of the complete work, under its definitive title, had to wait until April 1940, when Bartók himself played the piano part for the famous recording by Columbia with Szigeti and Goodman.

Contrasts is the odd man out among Bartók's chamber works. It is the only chamber music he ever wrote with a part for a wind instrument and – if one excludes the rather soloistic Rhapsodies – the only relatively light music among his works for instrumental ensemble. In this, something of the original rhapsody character suggested by Goodman obviously rubbed off on Bartók's inspiration. But even in the outer movements the dance spirit is stylised, and the material has little concrete resemblance to actual folk tunes. At times it rather recalls the earlier Bartók of the central movement of the First Violin Sonata, or the abstracted *verbunkos* tone of the Second, with its subtle thematic workmanship and acid harmonic colouring, but with the obvious difference that Bartók now makes all three parts do duty to the same material so that the title refers rather to contrasts of treatment and timbre than to a comprehensive clash of ideas such as we find in the violin sonatas. On the other hand the basic outlines of the *lassú-friss* sequence are plainer to see in *Contrasts*. In place of the rhapsodic opening movement of the romantic Hungarian pastiche (to which genre, in some respects, Bartók's own earlier essays also belong) he writes an authentic march-like 'recruiting dance' in *moderato* tempo but with a substantial measure of melodic embellishment in the authentic *verbunkos* style. The rapid ('*sebes*') Finale combines a typical *moto perpetuo* figuration with a touch of affectionate parody at the expense of the peasant fiddler performing on a mistuned instrument. To this Bartók adds just enough bravura in the cadenza for clarinet at the end of the first movement and the one for violin in the final section of the finale to evoke the traditional virtuoso manner of such dances. But the slow central movement (called '*Pihenö*' – 'relaxation') is more introverted in feeling, with almost nothing of the demonstrative *verbunkos* about it but a distinct resemblance to Bartók's recent nocturnal adagios, notably those in the Fifth Quartet and the *Sonata for two pianos and percussion*. Indeed the title strikes one as a misnomer; the music's restraint does more to charge the atmosphere with a tension which is only dissipated by the final dance.

Neither in form nor thematic character is *Contrasts* one of Bartók's most distinguished works. It strikes an at times uneasy balance between a jovial popular tone and an oblique and sophisticated harmonic language; between simple ternary forms marked by strong contrasts of mood, and a typically 'learned' motivic technique, leaning heavily on imitative points, mirror forms, and much of the contrapuntal apparatus of Bartók's mature style. It is nevertheless neat and effective in a good performance. The writing for violin and clarinet is idiomatic to a degree, and Bartók is able to profit from the fact that, of all the wind instruments, the clarinet is the one best equipped to swap blows with the violin in the sort of rippling close imitative work in which the Finale, especially, abounds. Moreover the music is rich in picturesque touches: the *scordatura* for the violin at the start of the Finale (the player has of course a second instrument to hand, duly mistuned with the E string on E flat and the G string on G sharp) added to the familiar Bartók repertory of string effects; and a whole range of impressionistic piano devices, including loud and soft *glissandi*, delicate bell-like clusters, tremolos and a kind of heterophonic unison style in the slow movement which Halsey Stevens considers to be derived from gamelan music (a genre mimicked also in a somewhat similar piece of *Mikrokosmos* called 'From the Island of Bali'). Stevens also regards the 'excessive' use of the tritone in *Contrasts* as an orientalism; he may have been misled by the exceptional purity of the treatment, particularly in 'Pihenö', since as we have seen the interval also pervades the *Sonata for two pianos*, to say nothing of the string quartets, in none of which works is there any exotic easternness (though no doubt many of the Magyarisms in Bartók's folk-song derivations are eastern in origin).

In any event the picturesque and varied character of *Contrasts* marks it as belonging to a new phase in Bartók's work, which eventually leads, via the Second Violin Concerto and the string

Divertimento to the more relaxed and extrovert works of his American years. His remaining works written in Europe have, admittedly, a streak of tragic melancholy not found either in *Contrasts* or in the American works but this was uniquely the consequence of the disruptive year 1939, which cost Bartók both his home and his mother, who died in December. The Sixth Quartet, Bartók's last major work before his emigration in October 1940, shares something of the heterogeneity of *Contrasts*; it even has some kinship of theme (the march themes of the two works are obviously related, and there is a fairly clear anticipation of the Quartet's 'Burletta' theme in the coda of the earlier work's Finale). Only the picture has been individualised, and a figure now moves in the landscape, unmistakably that of the bereft composer himself.

But Bartók only reintroduced himself gradually and, as it were, under force of circumstances. The most personal feature of the completed Sixth Quartet is the slow, motto-like music which prefaces each of the first three movements and emerges as the principal element of the last. This music, however, was apparently entirely absent from Bartók's original plan for the Quartet. He seems to have envisaged a somewhat dry four-movement scheme consisting (apparently) of the first three movements as we have them but without the prefatory slow music, together with a vigorous *moto perpetuo* Finale, of which he sketched some 90 bars before abandoning it. At some point, probably early in the composition of the 'Marcia' second movement, he conceived the idea of a motto introduction to each movement (including the original Finale: the sketches for this are preceded by the first 45 bars of the Mesto Finale as we now know it). Admittedly this motto may, as Benjamin Suchoff has observed, already have existed without being assigned a role in the Quartet, since jottings for it are to be found on the last page of the manuscript full score of the recently completed *Divertimento*, combined with the themes of the first two movements. But Bartók was still some way from realising the importance of the idea, and the change in the Finale came some time later, apparently after the completion of the other three movements.[1]

One can hardly refrain from relating this gradual change in the Quartet's perspective to changes in the surrounding circumstances

[1] Benjamin Suchoff, 'Structure and Concept in Bartók's Sixth Quartet', *Tempo*, no.83 (Winter 1967–8), pp.2–11. See also John Vinton, 'New Light on Bartók's Sixth Quartet', *Music Review*, XXV (1964), pp.224–238.

of Bartók's life. His initial work on the Quartet was done during August 1939 in a chalet near Saanen in the Bernese Oberland which Paul Sacher had put at his disposal while he was working on the *Divertimento* (another commission for Sacher's Basle Chamber Orchestra). But although Bartók's letters from Saanen echo the serenity and beauty of the environment, they also show that he was far from indifferent to the worsening situation outside. When the Soviet – German non-aggression pact was announced on 24 August, Bartók promptly returned to Budapest; he may well have had it in mind to emigrate forthwith (the possibility is already hinted at in his correspondence of 1938), but he was delayed by the illness of his mother, which grew worse during the autumn and led finally to her death just before Christmas. It was in this atmosphere of almost overpowering decline that the Sixth Quartet was at last finished in Novemeber. Writing from Naples the following April, Bartók told a Basle friend, Mrs Oscar Müller-Widman:

Three and a half months have passed since I lost my mother, and I still feel as if it had just happened yesterday. It is difficult to describe my state of mind which, in any case, it might perhaps be difficult for others to understand. However it is the self-reproaches that are most difficult to endure - all the things I should have done differently to make my mother's life easier and to comfort her in her last years. . . . Last summer, for instance, I went to Saanen to be totally undisturbed, so that I could write two works as quickly as possible; I spent three and a half weeks there, the works got done, wholly or in part, and those three and a half weeks I took away from my mother. I can never make amends for this. I should not have done it - and there were many similar things in the past - and none of this can be helped now.

A sense of regret for things past – whether to be helped or not – is certainly a powerful factor in the Sixth Quartet. It pervades the *mesto* theme on each occurrence, intensified by the scoring with solo viola sounding a melancholy note at the very start and muted *tremolo* upper strings sending an autumnal chill through the cello's variant in the second movement. The form of the last movement is particularly significant in this respect. Having suppressed the original *presto* music, Bartók continued (in bar 46) not with a new extension of the motto but with a fairly full allusion to each of the two main themes of the first movement, *molto tranquillo* and in a tempo reduced almost to that of the motto itself. The effect is radically different from that of the cyclic back-references in the Finales of the Fourth and Fifth Quartets. Here Bartók is not merely using a formal device to brace an arch structure; he is making his themes assume a quasi-dramatic role, to the extent that they rematerialise as characters remembered from some other context but now much altered, withered by time and sorrow, stripped of their erstwhile vitality and protean energy. This hallowed Romantic device is found hardly anywhere else in Bartók. Perhaps the 'con indifferenza' episode of the Fifth Quartet has something of the same self-dramatising, self-questioning property. But even there the music itself is thematic to the context in which it finds itself. The peculiar poignancy of the allusion in the Sixth Quartet is that it is not superficially apt at all; it is an uninvited guest at its own funeral.

Such images seem to have been far from Bartók's mind when he started work on the Sixth Quartet. Indeed it is precisely the sense of regret gradually undermining a set of initially vigorous ideas which gives the work its unique atmosphere and richness of experience. The *vivace* first movement, though less aggressive and a good deal smoother than its predecessors in the Fourth and Fifth Quartets, is in many ways the most alive of Bartók's sonata-form quartet movements, its vitality channelled into a brilliant repartee of themes and motives rather than into ebullient rhythmic gestures. In fact the slight rhythmic equivocation of the first theme, with its closing duplet-plus-fermata (pause) and the absence of any rhythmic accompaniment, provides the basis for one of Bartók's most plastic and mercurial pieces of string-writing, full of witty thematic puns (derived from the fact that the first subject is really a collection of three related three-note motives, *à la* Webern), and none the less mobile or harmonically diverse for the fact that rhythm and dissonance are treated with restraint (Ex. 23).

To compare such writing with even the best passages of Bartók's First Quartet, as has sometimes been done, is to reduce criticism to a handful of what Heinz-Klaus Metzger once called abortive concepts, such as 'romantically expressive', 'vaguely tonal' and so on. The Sixth Quartet is indeed tonal now and then (the first movement ends candidly in D major), in which respect it follows both the practice and the measure of recent works like the *Music for Strings*, the *Sonata for two pianos and percussion* and the Second Violin Concerto, where the harmonic language refers more openly than before to tonal types of chord but seldom uses Romantic chord progressions as such.[1]

[1] Some writers of a well-developed teleological tendency have even seen Bartók's six quartets as a kind of grand arch-form, curving up to the rarefied

Ex.23

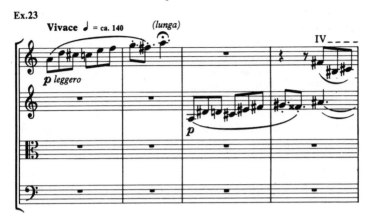

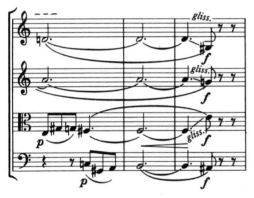

In these early stages the motto theme still seems destined for a subordinate role. The short viola solo leads thematically into a rhetorical unison passage (whose similarity to the opening of Beethoven's *Grosse Fuge* has often been remarked) which soon becomes an augmented version of the first subject in the Vivace. In each of the first three movements Bartók contrives an appropriate motivic transition from the motto theme to the theme of the

heights of the Third and Fourth Quartets before descending once again, not without a sigh of relief, to its Romantic origins. On this view the Seventh Quartet which Bartók is said to have sketched would probably have been a piece of neo-juvenilia.

movement proper (the second violin's tag which announces the 'Marcia' theme is apparently taken from the fifth bar of the motto, while the same instrument's rising phrase leading to the 'Burletta' theme is simply a reply to the descending sequence which closes the motto). But at the same time the motto itself grows in both size and significance. Its length increases from 13 bars to 16½ to 20 and finally 45 bars (of slightly slower tempo), and with each recurrence one 'real' part is added: in the second movement a descant played by unison violins and viola, in the third two contrapuntal parts with the tune (first violin) later doubled by the viola, and in the fourth three independent contrapuntal parts. The effect of all this is naturally to lend increasing emotional tension to the context of each successive movement. Where the Vivace was simply a sonata Allegro with a reflective slow introduction, the Marcia already has the flavour of one of those bitter Mahlerian marches in which the strutting and bravado are merely a cover for some deep misery, while the Burletta, a grotesque folk dance such as is found quite often in Bartók's earlier music (not always with a savage or ironic intention), has here a bitter, caustic taste, emphasised by the strident down-bows of the second bar, the gritty heel-of-the-bow ('*au talon*') of the other bars, and the rending quarter-tone mistunings on the violins' *glissando* figure in bar 6 (26 of the whole movement). Special effects abound in these central movements. The banshee wailing of the cello on its A-string in the trio section of the Marcia (especially bar 94 *et seq.*) is one of Bartók's most extraordinary touches (Ex. 24), apparently based on a distortion of that very *parlando rubato* folk-music style which produced the pure expression of the central movement in the Fourth Quartet.

Ex.24

Against it the viola plays strummed pizzicato chords with agitated tremolo in the violins. One could also mention the use of pizzicato *glissando* in the reprise of the Burletta and the rapid alternation of pizzicato and *saltando* ('jump-bowing'), along with sudden changes of dynamic and a 'thrown' rhythmic stress which occasionally recalls Stravinsky (there is an obvious similarity between the passage starting at bar 46 of the Burletta and the fiddle tune in Stravinsky's *Soldier's Tale*, Ex. 25 overleaf).

The form and development of these movements is by Bartók's standards quite uncomplicated. They are scarcely more than ternary-form character-pieces; or a pair of successive scherzos-with-trios. Yet they exhibit Bartók's usual meticulous care over architectural detail. The Marcia is almost entirely formed out of the opening arpeggio-plus-scale figure of the main theme together with variants of its characteristic dotted rhythm (this is the theme so clearly prefigured in the first movement of *Contrasts*). Even the *risoluto* second theme, though its character is sturdier, comes simply from an extension of the march's rising scale and soon dissolves back into it, while the remaining new idea (second violin, bar 58 etc.) is in effect a descant over an ostinato-like discussion of the arpeggio march motive. In the recapitulation some of this material is inverted (notably the Risoluto), though not apparently according to any pattern. The Burletta also derives most of its ideas from an arpeggio figure in the main theme (see especially bar 25 onwards) together with the rhythms and special colouring (down-bows, *glissandi*, mistunings) which go with it. As in the march, isolated thirds (major or minor) are important, taken from the arpeggios; and again the trio

Ex.25

section (bar 70) is more lyrical, but this time without parody – the compound quavers of the *andantino* melody vaguely recall the motto theme, and at bar 78 there is a fleeting reminiscence of the choriambic second subject of the first movement (bar 81). Fragments of this material return at the end of the movement by way of coda, but are quickly shut out by the Burletta theme.

The valedictory finale, with its central allusions to the first movement, also has a ternary structure, on paper. But what is perhaps more significant is that for the first time the *mesto* theme is itself developed within its initial statement, and moreover that this development was already present in the version Bartók wrote as introduction to the later discarded *presto*. Instead of simply lengthening and modifying the theme, Bartók first takes the opening phrase alone, varies it, then inserts a lengthy contrapuntal development of this idea (bars 13 to 30) before completing the statement of the motto itself more or less in its original form. This whole passage is therefore a good deal weightier than any previous version of the motto, and it is not very surprising that, on consideration, Bartók felt that a farther Allegro movement would be both redundant and disrupting. What remains is little more than an extended coda, with the first movement reminiscence leading to a mere shadow of a reprise of the motto, a few disjointed gestures of (perhaps) protest, and a shrug of resignation from the cello.

It would be no compliment to Bartók to say that the Sixth Quartet sums up his life's work in the medium of the string quartet. Genius, when it is not actually moribund, necessarily moves on – and that Bartók's genius was very far from moribund is shown by the astonishing vitality of the American works, the *Concerto for orchestra* the *Sonata for solo violin*, and the Third Piano Concerto, none of which in any way reflects either the bleak sorrow of his final months in Europe or the struggle and illness of his life in the States. But though the Sixth Quartet is a strikingly different sort of work from any of its predecessors, a work in which conflicting emotions have to some extent disturbed the fine organisation and balance of the Fourth and Fifth Quartets, the *Music for Strings* or the *Sonata for two pianos*, it remains a masterly exhibition of the technical and expressive possibilities of a genre which, as history shows, has always refused to be limited to this or that type of utterance. Bartók's handling of the medium and of his ideas is here as assured as it ever was. The rigorous motivic fabric and the by now effortless treatment of academic contrapuntal procedures, combined with a somewhat more plastic approach to rhythm than before, give the first movement, at least, an almost god-like vitality and completeness which it shares with the first movement of the *Sonata for two pianos*, and the second of the *Music for Strings*. The lightness of touch is a sure sign of the master, as in late Beethoven. If the later movements upset this serenity, they still do so within a brilliant and apt handling of the medium. Nowhere is Bartók's sense of what is possible with four strings more acute than in the central movements of the Sixth Quartet. As for the music's harmonic resource, we may call the work tonal but only on the understanding that this does not imply any restriction of means. The point about Bartók's late tonal music is that it absorbs the wide range of his earlier dissonant practices, whether polymodal, motivic or purely linear, into a language which once again acknowledges harmonic repose in the traditional sense. So the dissonances of the Sixth Quartet may be less strident or startling than those of the Third, Fourth or even Fifth, but they are hardly less free-ranging. An examination of the development sections of the first movement (for instance bar 60 *et seq.*) or the Marcia and Burletta in general will show that the change is mainly one of emphasis.

Writers on Bartók's chamber music have tried in various ways to characterise its achievement as they see it. For some it is the fusion of Eastern (Magyar) and Western (classical) elements into a new synthesis; for others it is the revitalisation of the great Beethoven tradition, the reassertion of the high classical values of form and intellect, and the sublimation of emotion in a medium whose character is essentially pure. Some like to regard Bartók's quartets as in some sense a symbol or embodiment of the best in everything he wrote. Some see them as an intimate diary, others as a barely contained struggle between warring elements. Curiously none of these assessments seems in any fundamental way untrue, though some may seem rather to miss the point. It is the variety of admiring response they command which is perhaps the best testimonial to the comprehensive power of these great works.

Index of Main Works